Achieving Excellence

SMB Practices in Turbulent Times

By

Alex Boussetta

i

Acknowledgements

Within these chapters, a constellation of leaders and their collectives shine brightly. I am deeply grateful to each one of them for igniting the spark of inspiration that guided this book—especially Gilles Beaulne, Daniel Blanche, Eric Martel, Minh Dat Nguyen, Saibal Ray, Eric Saine, Anoop Singh, and Serge Varin, whose very essence fueled the creation of these pages. They generously shared their insights, experiences, and visions for a better future.

I also want to express my heartfelt appreciation to my partner in life, Catharina Deer, and to my steadfast companions, Steve Craney, David Lapointe, and Martin Auger Rochon, for walking alongside me on this path. They supported me with their encouragement, feedback, and friendship throughout this journey.

And to Sara Infantino—a resounding tribute for her wisdom, imaginative spirit, meticulous research, and invaluable suggestions that shaped the genesis of this book. She was instrumental in bringing this project to fruition.

Contents

Chapter 1 – Introduction

We often hear statements reflecting a sense of resignation, claims that individuals no longer care about their workplaces, that companies cannot improve, or that people are too disengaged to go beyond their regular duties, even in cases of emergency. These sentiments have been echoed by numerous sources, including colleagues at McGill University, where I have been teaching for over two decades, and clients our consulting firm has served for 15 years. They consistently express challenges in performing well, pleasing customers and retaining staff. This narrative indicates an impending collapse.

However, is this truly the reality? I invite you, the reader, to consider this question yourself.

Consider the evidence: restaurants shutting down due to staff shortages, airlines like WestJet reducing flights because of pilot scarcity, social service agencies experiencing 70% annual employee turnover rates, aerospace giants like Boeing losing critical expertise, and major consulting firms like PWC, KPMG, EY, and Deloitte facing large-scale layoffs not only from business shrinkage but also from unmet client expectations (1).

The data below comes from Gallup (2).

According to Gallup, employees in the U.S. feel more detached from their employers, with less clear expectations, lower levels of satisfaction with their organization, and less connection to its mission or purpose than they did four years ago. They are also less likely to feel someone at work cares about them as a person.

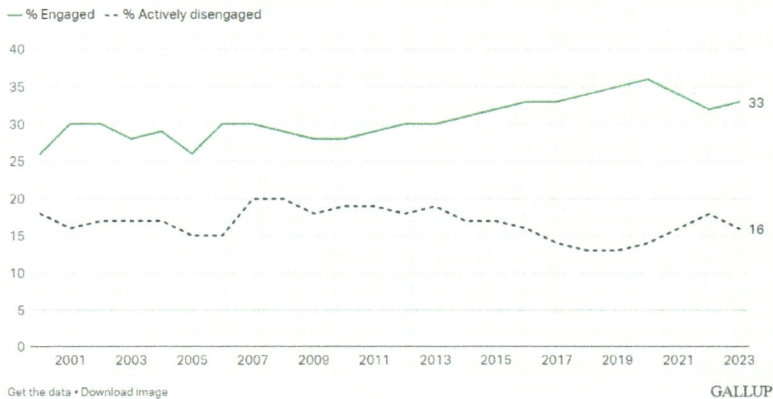

Employee Engagement 2023, Gallup

In Canada, in 2023, 60% of employees are not engaged, 15% are actively disengaged at work, and only 25% are actively engaged (3).

One might argue that these numbers in Canada and the U.S. are higher than in many countries, and that is correct. Nevertheless, there is an opportunity to reconcile this engagement with the organization's performance and ability to deliver to customers.

Despite these challenges, we remain optimistic that with the right mindset and strategy – focusing on total people engagement – we can reverse this trend.

There are numerous examples of companies that have flourished during these challenging times, achieving both remarkable performance and high employee satisfaction. Companies such as Aldo Shoes have rebounded from bankruptcy, Laurentide Controls excels in industrial services, Van Houtte Coffee Services thrives in catering and rentals, the Region of Peel delivers exceptional municipal services, and CDMV shines in veterinary supply distribution.

These success stories include small to medium-sized businesses (SMBs) that have embraced principles such as adaptability, agility, continuous improvement, and proactive listening to both customer and employee feedback.

This book aims to provide value to SMBs across various sectors—including service, manufacturing, social services, and healthcare—by outlining the key values, behaviours, methodologies, and tools necessary for success amidst adversity. However, it is also applicable to larger organizations.

This book is designed for business leaders, entrepreneurs, specialists in improvement, and agents of transformation and change eager to discover strategies for advancing people development and engagement.

Expertise in improvement methodologies such as Lean, Lean Six Sigma, and Kaizen is not required to appreciate the findings and tools that will be presented.

We begin by examining the current landscape through the lenses of employees, customers, and technology. We then discuss the unique position of SMBs in comparison to corporate behemoths concerning funding, recruitment, and market dynamics.

A step-by-step improvement roadmap is introduced, which includes a rapid MBA-like primer on business basics.

The journey through this roadmap involves several stages. Initially focusing on the value delivered to the customer, followed by cultivating a profound comprehension of core business practices, and a collaborative review of operational techniques.

Subsequently, we aim to elevate the consistency of employee and customer experiences via redesign. Only then can optimization ensue, concentrating on enhancing performance and striving for industry leadership.

Lastly, we explore methods to anticipate and tailor responses to each customer request with finesse and specificity.

We provide numerous examples throughout to illustrate the suggested practices and plenty of diagrams and graphs to visualize the notions discussed.

(1) The Big Con: How the Consulting Industry Weakens Our Businesses, Infantilizes Our Governments, and Warps Our Economies, Mariana Mazzucato
(2) https://www.gallup.com/workplace/608675/new-workplace-employee-engagement-stagnates.aspx
(3) https://www.canadahrcentre.com/solutions/employee-engagement/

Chapter 2 - What is Different Today?

Well, to be honest, everything has changed, and every single business practice could be challenged!

Although this is true, this would not be a very practical way to look at things. In this chapter, we will be focusing on describing some key elements that business managers need to be aware of and reflect on.

Understanding, Engaging, and Motivating the New Generations

The evolving landscape of the modern workplace brings with it the challenge of understanding and motivating a new breed of employees. Millennials and Generation Z, with their unique characteristics and expectations, have prompted a re-evaluation of traditional motivational strategies. Millennials and Generation Z are characterized by their technological savvy, adaptability, and a global perspective. Raised in an era of rapid technological advancements and social media, these generations are well-connected, value diversity, and are more environmentally and socially conscious than their predecessors. For these younger workers, a job is not just a means to an end but an integral part of their identity and life. They seek workplaces that provide more than just financial rewards; work-life balance, flexibility, and a sense of purpose are crucial. They prefer environments where they feel valued and heard and where there is a clear alignment between their personal values and the company's mission.

Some companies have followed these guidelines for decades. Let us take the example of General Electric. Having been multiple times to their facilities located in Louisville, KY. The first time I went to this facility, I met James, a senior marketing director at the time, and Mary, who held the position of marketing director. James, a Black man, and Mary, a Chinese woman, stood out for their uncommon representation. In 1994, it was unusual to find individuals from diverse cultural backgrounds, particularly women, occupying such high-ranking positions.

This has created a competitive advantage for General Electric exceedingly early on. I have met and interacted with many of their senior managers who come from quite diverse racial, cultural, and gender backgrounds. This diversity helped create a truly varied pool of ideas and creativity.

Furthermore, as part of product development activities, design reviews are essential to provide feedback and identify opportunities for improvement on new designs. The participants in these design reviews consisted of multi-functional team members, senior consulting experts, and a fresh pair of eyes coming from new recruits. Everyone was invited to provide comments and share their opinions. As a young engineer, it provided me with a sense of belonging and contribution to these challenging projects, developing brand-new solutions for consumers. In my engineering role, despite being one of the younger members, I was invited to contribute to tasks that extended beyond my technical expertise. This provided me with the opportunity to gain experience in sales, marketing, and finance which allowed me to fully understand how these functions integrate and relate to each other. Several other companies, including Pratt and Whitney, Ubisoft, and Google, have adopted this strategy early on to promote learning and engage new employees. In the good years of BlackBerry, when their products were still highly sought after, more than twenty different languages were spoken by our quality management team.

So, what are some ways to motivate them?

- Career growth and learning opportunities are vital for motivating these generations. They are eager to develop their skills and appreciate mentorship and continuous learning opportunities. Organizations that invest in their employees' growth can expect higher levels of engagement and loyalty.

- The traditional 9-to-5 workday is less appealing to these groups. Flexibility in work hours and the option for remote work are not just perks but expected. This flexibility is seen as a sign of trust and respect, leading to increased job satisfaction and productivity.

- Millennials and Gen Z are motivated by work that has a positive impact on society and aligns with their personal values. Companies that can articulate how their employees' work contributes to the greater good will find it easier to motivate and retain these workers.

- Recognition for these generations goes beyond monetary rewards. They value personalized, meaningful recognition that reflects their contributions. Creative rewards, public acknowledgement, and opportunities for advancement can be more motivating than traditional incentives.

Regular, constructive feedback and open lines of communication are essential. These generations thrive on knowing where they stand and how they can improve. Regular check-ins and a culture of open dialogue resonate with their desire for growth and recognition.

- Understand and adapt to their leadership approach, for example, the importance of value authenticity and transparency.

- As leaders and managers, we understand that we need to walk the talk and lead by example. These generations prefer leaders who show the way and are hands-on and truthful to what has been said.

However, one of the biggest challenges is balancing the diverse needs and expectations of a multi-generational workforce. Creating an inclusive culture that values the inputs and preferences of all generations is key. This includes offering a range of benefits and working styles to cater to different preferences.

Motivating employees from new generations requires a nuanced understanding of their unique characteristics and aspirations. Strategies that emphasize personal development, work-life balance, purposeful work, innovative recognition, and effective communication are essential. As the workplace continues to evolve, organizations that successfully engage with these newer generations will find themselves at the forefront of innovation and productivity, harnessing the full potential of a diverse and dynamic workforce.

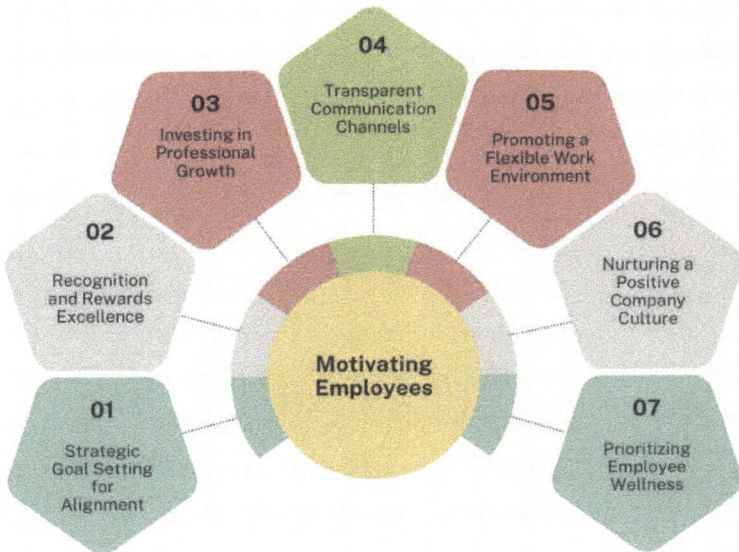

Motivating employees

Customer Expectations

Customer expectations have evolved at an alarming speed since the pandemic. Here are a few examples related to the current expectations. It might be argued that some are reasonable. Let us, however, remember the old proverb: the customer is king. We need to understand "the Voice of the Customer" – what they want, what they think, how they feel, and how they want to feel.

- Increased Demand for Fast Delivery: With a surge in online shopping, many customers have shown impatience regarding delivery times. Expectations for same-day or next-day deliveries have increased, with customers often expressing frustration over any delays.

- Shorter Wait Time Tolerance: In retail and service industries, customers have shown less tolerance for waiting, be it in lines, for service, or for back-ordered products. The accustomed convenience and speed of online services have heightened expectations for rapid service in physical locations.

- Impatience with Technology Glitches: As more interactions move online, customers show less patience for technological issues during virtual meetings, online shopping, or customer service interactions. Even minor technical problems often result in significant frustration.

- Response Time on Customer Service Inquiries: There has been a noticeable impatience for quick responses to customer service inquiries, whether through email, chat, or social media. Customers expect almost immediate replies, reflecting a broader trend of decreased patience in digital communication.

In the healthcare sector, these expectations evolved even more, occasionally resulting in unfortunate violence. For instance, one patient's husband broke a doctor's leg in Perth, Ontario. A staff member in Smiths Falls, ON, was stabbed in the head with a pair of scissors. A nurse was nearly strangled at a hospital in Montreal (2.1).

Here is a summary of the main changes in the healthcare sector:

- Increased Demand for Immediate Services: After experiencing rapid response and urgency during the pandemic, people might have developed higher expectations for quick healthcare services. They may feel impatient with longer waiting times for appointments or slower responses.

- Telemedicine Adaptation: Many have become accustomed to the convenience of telemedicine during the pandemic. Post-pandemic, people might feel impatient with the need to physically visit clinics for issues that could be addressed virtually, perceiving it as a waste of time.

- Mental Health Services: There was a surge in mental health issues due to the pandemic, leading to increased demand for these services. People might experience impatience due to long waiting lists or insufficient availability of mental health professionals.

- Expectation of Efficiency: The pandemic forced healthcare systems to adapt and become more efficient in many areas. Post-pandemic, patients may have less tolerance for perceived inefficiencies, such as redundant paperwork, repetitive questioning, or delays in treatment.

Let us take the example of the Canadian Mental Health Association, which needed to reinvent itself during the COVID-19 lockdown and after the lockdown. Typical mental health clients seeking support and needing to register for programs related to stress, depression, addiction, and other mental health concerns are typically approached through face-to-face appointments. Group therapy, for example, would be conducted in meeting rooms in very accessible places. Following the lockdown, The Canadian Mental Health Association needed to implement drastic measures in terms of offering its services, as face-to-face appointments were no longer an option. These were first offered by phone and through video Conference Services. After a few months, as the world started to reopen, CMHA could have just cancelled all those online services and gone back to a traditional face-to-face setting. The CMHA decided against discontinuing these services and continued to offer them, which were now highly appreciated by clients. Several surveys were launched to clients to ask about their preferred communication methods, including some methods that were not used previously. An example of a discovery made from the surveys is the importance of texting, which is one of the preferred methods for teenagers. That relentless focus on *the voice of the customer* made their success and reputation.

Management Skills

Traditionally, management on-the-job training and formal education have mostly focused on understanding the work to be done, including its constraints in terms of customer expectations, quality, costs, and expected deadlines. This strategy makes perfect sense in a hierarchical setting where roles and responsibilities are determined by the organizational chart. In many instances, process experts and high performers in terms of delivery are promoted to the management levels. This is what is highlighted on the diagram below in green. A second focus is made on driving accountability in each organizational team. The ultimate accountability remains at the management level, as they are the ones to allocate priorities and resources.

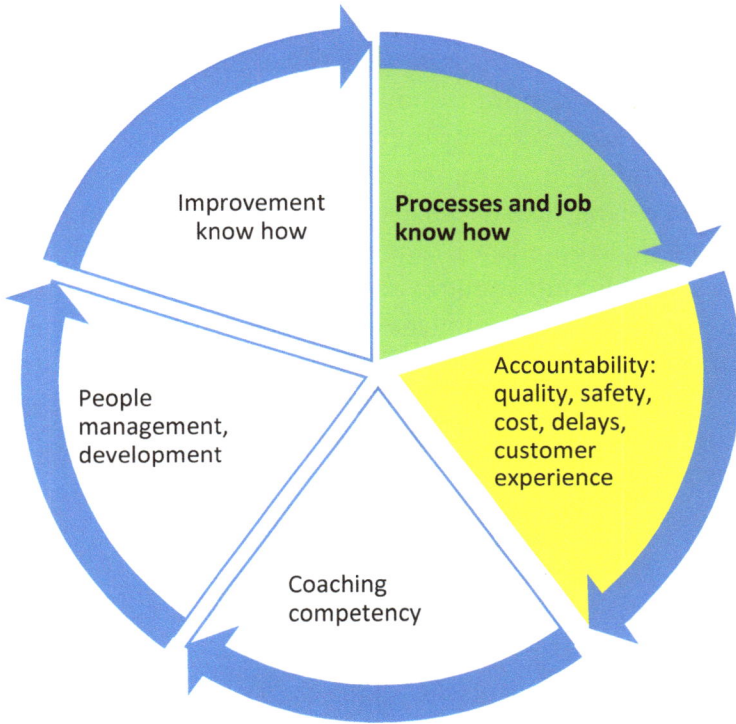

Management Competencies

This focus has shifted as employees are not regarded as human resources or assets anymore. This change of focus has been described by David Norton and Robert Kaplan (2.2). Human resources used to be qualified as intangible assets, meaning that their presence and involvement are necessary but not related to the worth of an organization. This mindset creates a gap in terms of how much is invested in intangible assets, such as growth, personal development, and training. They are, in fact, the most important aspect of an organization. They are tangible, can be measured, and quantified. Intangible assets include people, information, and customer relationships, and they are all critical to the success of an organization.

People represent the most significant asset of any organization and can drive quicker and more thorough performance and execution within the organization rather than relying solely on a commend-and-control strategy from top management. Therefore, the focus has shifted to driving accountability at all levels of the organization and ensuring that there is a strong collaboration among all levels. For managers, this shift requires strong people management and development skills. The employees are regarded as the ultimate drivers of performance and process completion. We will discuss later the ripple effect that these have on the training that managers require in terms of improvement methodologies, tools, and coaching competencies.

Management competencies today

Technology and the Digital Age

Finally, the day is coming when writing is fading away. Typing and voice-to-text are the norm. Countries such as the USA and Finland have removed cursive writing from their school curriculums. Statistics are scarce on the percentage of the population who have forgotten how to handwrite. However, I personally encountered a dozen situations in Canada, the USA, and China where young students could not write down an address with a pen and needed to type it on their smartphones.

This trend, though, has an interesting benefit. Every word and thought has become digitized and accessible for lookups, enabling tools such as ChatGPT to process an infinite array of inputs. Office automation tools can thrive and are becoming increasingly accurate. In combination with lower costs for data processing of any kind, including servers, personal computers, and smartphones, these automation tools are getting cheaper and more affordable for organizations of any size.

The digital age is making information processing so easy that it makes it bearable to work with inefficient processes. When comparing technology and process design, the burden of bureaucracy becomes less painful. Moreover, we can see what these can lead to. Let us share an interesting example from an aerospace company we work with. An expense approval used to take four months to gather the required seventeen signatures. With workflow automation, this approval process now takes three weeks to gather the seventeen digital approvals. People were happy. After a process review, the seventeen approvals were dropped to three, and it is now taking two days. Great combination of automation and process design. We made and experimented and attempted to navigate the approval process without automation. Instead of two days, it took five days.

This raises the question: if we have limited time and resources, should we automate or redesign the process first? Or, as Shakespeare would have put it in Hamlet Act III, Scene I, to automate or not to automate, that is the question! It depends on the investment needed, of course. Still, as we can see in the table below, the improvement rates are quite steeper for process redesign.

	No Process redesign	Process redesign
No Automation	120 days Baseline	5 days 24-fold improvement
Automation	21 days 6-fold improvement	2 days 60-fold improvement

Process redesign vs automation

The example given is related to office automation. However, it is still applicable to any type of robotization or process automation in the domains of healthcare, manufacturing, and others. We will be covering other examples in the next parts related to best practices in processors and people and then introducing automation and advanced technologies.

We will also be covering in the next chapters the advantages and disadvantages of automation, such as having the right flexibility in terms of new customer needs and new variants of a process that need to be used or developed. Here is a brief list for consideration:

A few advantages:

- Increased Productivity: Automation can speed up processes and eliminate the need for manual labour, resulting in increased output and shorter production cycles.

- Improved Accuracy and Quality: Automation can perform tasks with precision and consistency, resulting in higher-quality of products or services. It can also reduce human errors and defects.

- Enhanced Efficiency and Cost Savings: Automation can optimize workflows, eliminate bottlenecks, and reduce wastage of time and resources. It can also lower labour costs and operational expenses.

- Increased Safety for Equipment and Machinery Automation: It can replace humans in tasks that pose risks to human safety, such as hazardous work environments. It can minimize the occurrence of accidents, injuries, and occupational hazards.

- Scalability and Flexibility: Automation can be easily scaled up or down to accommodate changes in demand. It can also adjust production levels, allocate resources, and respond to market fluctuations quickly.

A few nasty disadvantages:

- Job Displacement and Unemployment: Automation can replace human workers in many tasks and processes, resulting in the potential loss of jobs and income for many people. This can have negative social and economic impacts, such as increased poverty, inequality, and social unrest. Initial Implementation Costs: Automation can require a high capital investment to design, fabricate, and install automated systems. This can be a barrier for small and medium-sized businesses or for developing countries, to adopt automation technologies.

- Technical Challenges and Limitations: Automation can face technical issues, such as malfunctions, breakdowns, cyberattacks, or power outages, which can disrupt the production process and cause losses or damages. Automation can also have limitations in terms of flexibility, adaptability, and creativity compared to human workers.

- Reduced Human Interaction and Customer Experience: Automation can reduce the need for human interaction and communication in the workplace, which can affect the social and emotional well-being of workers and customers. Automation can also affect the customer experience, as some customers may prefer human contact and personalization over automated services.

- Dependency on Technology and Loss of Human Skills: Automation can create a dependency on technology and machinery, which can make humans less capable of performing tasks and processes without them. Automation can also lead to the loss of human skills and knowledge, as humans may become less involved in the learning and decision-making processes.

Automation and ethics are two topics that are closely entwined nowadays. As discussed in the previous examples, the search for efficiency, effectiveness and productivity does not lead to only one avenue, the roadmap does not only consist of tools and automation.

This chapter was an introduction to what needs to be considered today and why we cannot rely on cookie-cutter approaches that have been working for decades!

References

2.1   https://macleans.ca/longforms/er-doctor-healthcare-crisis-canada/

2.2 The balanced scorecard, Kaplan, Norton, 1992

Chapter 3 – Small and Midsize Businesses and Corporate Giants

What do we mean by a small, medium, or large business? What are their key differences in terms of their landscape, and how does this affect their survival and growth?

Small vs. Big Enough vs. Very Big

First, a small business is characterized by having fewer than 100 employees, while a medium-sized business falls within the range of 100 to 500 employees, and a large business typically exceeds 500 employees.

The figures below show us the importance of those small businesses in Canada and in the USA. In both countries, we can see that they represent 98 percent or more of the total number of businesses. In 2021, there were approximately 1.2 million small businesses in Canada and 32 million of them in the USA. These numbers show the changing trends in terms of entrepreneurship and risk appetite.

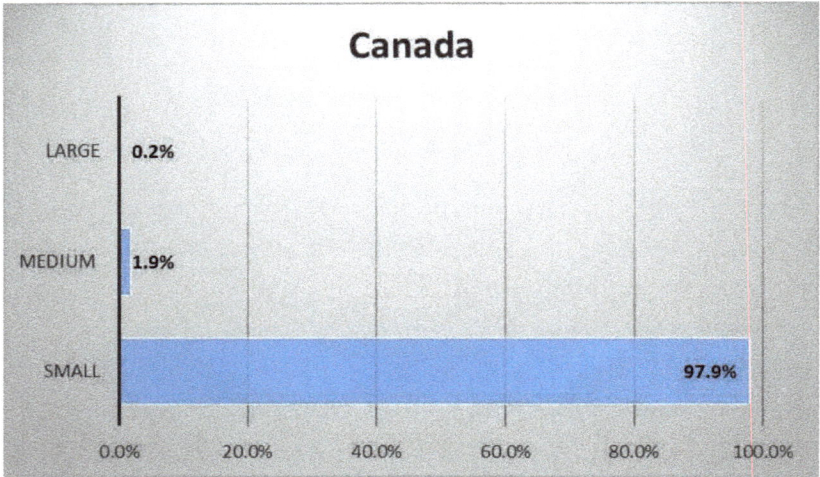

Canada

LARGE	0.2%
MEDIUM	1.9%
SMALL	97.9%

0.0%   20.0%   40.0%   60.0%   80.0%   100.0%

Business size ratios in Canada, 2021

Innovation, Science and Economic Development Canada, Key Small Business Statistics (1)

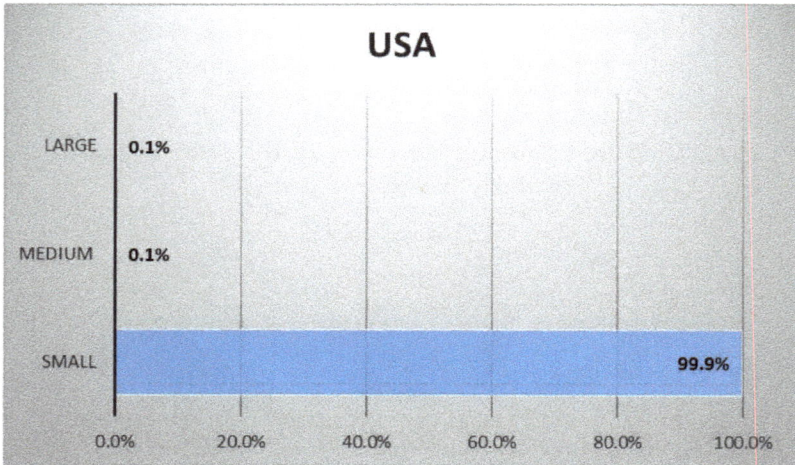

USA

LARGE	0.1%
MEDIUM	0.1%
SMALL	99.9%

0.0%   20.0%   40.0%   60.0%   80.0%   100.0%

Business size ratios in USA, 2021

Innovation, Science and Economic Development Canada, Key Small Business Statistics (1)

This is a very compelling image, showing how many small-scale enterprises are providing services and goods which are very often customized for a diverse population. However, ensuring survival for these types of businesses is very challenging for multiple reasons that will be discussed. As we see on the next chart, 26% of small businesses have already disappeared after five years. The chart presented focuses on businesses that have at least 20 employees, as the survival rates of the other ones are much lower.

Many factors contribute to these closures. Of course, they are related primarily to cash flow, profitability, difficulties in getting resources and keeping these resources engaged. These factors will be explored below.

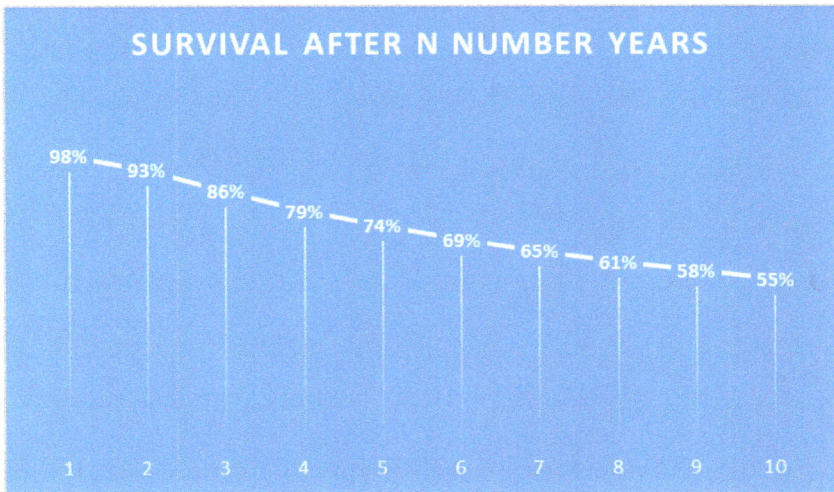

SURVIVAL AFTER N NUMBER YEARS

98% — 93% — 86% — 79% — 74% — 69% — 65% — 61% — 58% — 55%

1   2   3   4   5   6   7   8   9   10

Survival of small business (from 20 to 100 employees)

Innovation, Science and Economic Development Canada, Key Small Business Statistics (1)

Attracting Employees and Living Up to Their Expectations

Small and midsize businesses (SMBs) face several challenges when it comes to hiring employees.

First, competition from larger companies. Small businesses often must compete with larger companies that can offer better salaries and benefits. Depending on where the company is in terms of its growth and establishing a stable customer base, resources will be limited, and they might not be able to provide better salaries without accepting a certain risk. Working with a community service agency focused on the senior population in Toronto; they mentioned to me that they were looking to fill an entry-level social worker position. They were targeting a $85,000 salary. Although they liked the job description, most candidates took the job down, mentioning that large pharmaceutical companies were also targeting social workers and were offering a minimum of $120,000.

Employment seekers' behaviours do follow the pillars of the Maslow pyramid, job security and compensation first. Job seekers would sort and choose where to apply based on those initial criteria. Although the size of a corporation does not guarantee any type of security, there is still a perception that a longstanding presence in a large corporation implies greater job security and longer-term employment opportunities. Perceptions... of employees might be seen as pure numbers or assets in these large corporations. This hiring issue becomes an exponential problem when specialized resources are needed. Specialized technicians, accounts, engineers, and programmers need a development plan and challenges. Interactions during the hiring process with the business owners and managers become crucial, although they may not have the time to devote to recruiting and hiring new employees while also managing other aspects of their business.

Many job seekers look for brand recognition and would rather go with a well-known firm where they think that their contribution would be much more significant. Branding and clarity of a corporation's purpose become paramount. Is it feasible for a small corporation to provide this clarity?

As an example, let's look at Support Senior Persons Living Connected: https://www.splc.ca.

Mission: Understand the aspirations of seniors and respond with innovative support.

Vision: Building inclusive communities where all seniors are connected to living their best possible lives.

Or Laurentide Controls, https://www.laurentide.com

Purpose: Our purpose is to help industry thrive in Eastern Canada. As an entirely employee-owned company, every member of our team is driven by the shared goal of empowering people and advancing the industry.

These sentences are engaging and very clear. The mention of a company's mission and mission on an employment posting or during an interview can drastically change the interest level of candidates.

Flexibility

Another critical difference between SMBs and large corporations is the flexibility needed. Having a large customer base such as Salesforce or Shopify generates a financial buffer. Even if 30% of customers would walk away, there is enough volume and customer dependency to ensure the company's viability for years. Eventually, these large corporations would also need to turn around and pursue new products and services. Depending on how this planning is done, this sometimes forces organizations to cannibalize other product lines to survive. We can think of all the automotive corporations, such as Ford or Toyota, who needed to inject electrical vehicles into their portfolio to appeal to a new rising segment of customers. There are multiple ways to manage this type of flexibility or agility, and having the right structure and values in place would engender a better profitability and survival rate overall. Think for one moment of the Kodak Corporation who decided not to react to the emergence of digital photography, even though Kodak was the inventor of that technology!

For small companies such as CDMV as an example, (https://www.cdmv.com), a distributor of veterinary supplies, flexibility is a challenge and an opportunity. CDMV is doing very well due to its dedicated listening to the voice of the customer and adapting to new challenges and requirements. As an example, agreements were signed with major pharmaceutical companies to streamline the delivery of medication to animal clinics and hospitals and more efficient supply chain flows were established.

We will be discussing how to create this flexibility, which is also referred to as agility. There are some basic principles that can be applied that enable low-cost adaptation to those types of opportunities and situations.

Infrastructure

In relation to these flexibility principles, the infrastructure becomes a significant element. An infrastructure might be seen as a multi-dimensional beast as it has roots in the cost structure as well as in the human structure.

In terms of cost structure, a high level of investment in fixed costs, such as break-and-mortar buildings, working space, warehouses, equipment and machinery, and computers, do create edgy pendants on what was established and the types of products and services that the company offers. Although multiple physical resources are available, a turnaround to other projects and services might be very difficult. Take, for example, a clothing company that invested heavily in fabric cutting and sewing technology. Changing from one type of sewing or from one type of fabric to the other might be a challenge as the equipment might not be appropriate to fit new needs, such as going from a short production to a furniture fabric production.

Moreover, a focus on variable costs, rather than fixed costs, might be preferred, such as working with a network of partners and third parties, leasing equipment, and focusing more on processes and configurable tools than on machinery.

Another side of infrastructure is the organizational chart or the way that human resources are arranged. A tall pyramid style does ensure direction and compliance with goals. However, communication might be indirect and slow in terms of decision-making and escalating risks that could affect the execution. An unfortunate, well-known example is the Space Shuttle Challenger in 1986. The experts at the bottom of the pyramid knew about the issue related to an O-Ring but had no means to communicate a clear message to the top of the pyramid. This resulted in poor decision-making in terms of the risk assessment, and the shuttle took off and broke apart after 73 seconds, killing everyone on board.

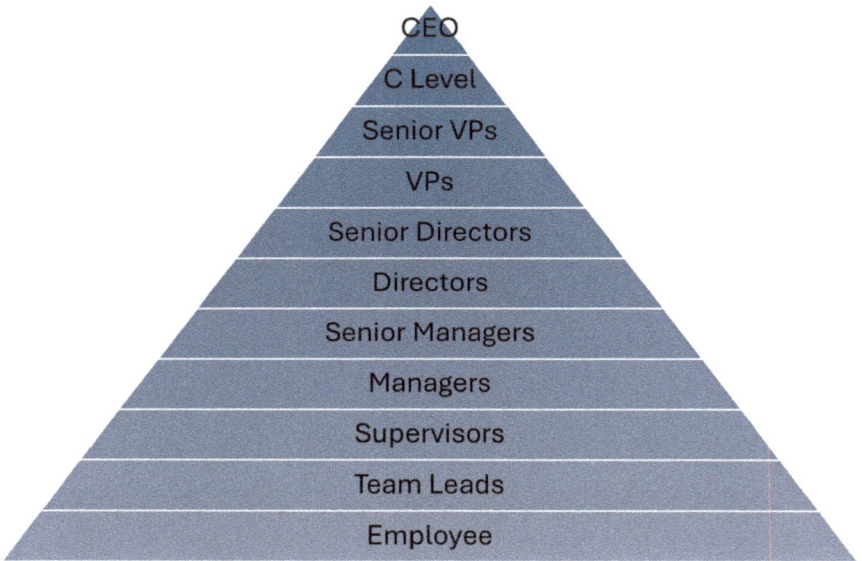

Tall Pyramid

A shallow type of pyramid structure ensures quicker and more direct communication in terms of success, failure, and risk mitigation.

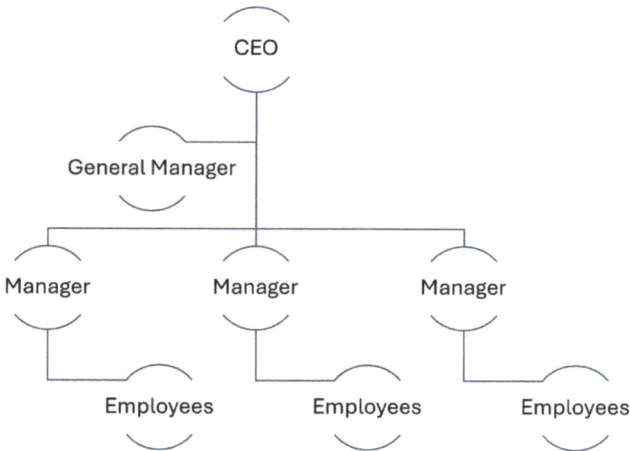

Shallow Pyramid

25

Cash and Funding

It would be a very exhausting and long task to list all the ways that the company can raise funding. We could write another book about it! Going from issuing shares, bonds, credit lines and mortgages through venture capital firms, and quote a few other ways to do it.

For a private organization, whatever the size, it always takes weeks or months of negotiation regarding the terms and conditions. Looking for governmental grants should be one of the first steps to getting grants or securing a loan with low interest rates.

As discussed earlier in this chapter, the smaller the organization, the lower the survival rate. As we can see on the chart below, cash is the second most important reason. Hence, managing the cash flow, meaning how much money is available in the bank account is paramount. A company could survive if it has enough cash, even though it is not profitable for many years. For example, Uber is still not profitable at the time that we are writing this book! We will be discussing in another chapter about cash flow practices that will commonly also refer to as working capital.

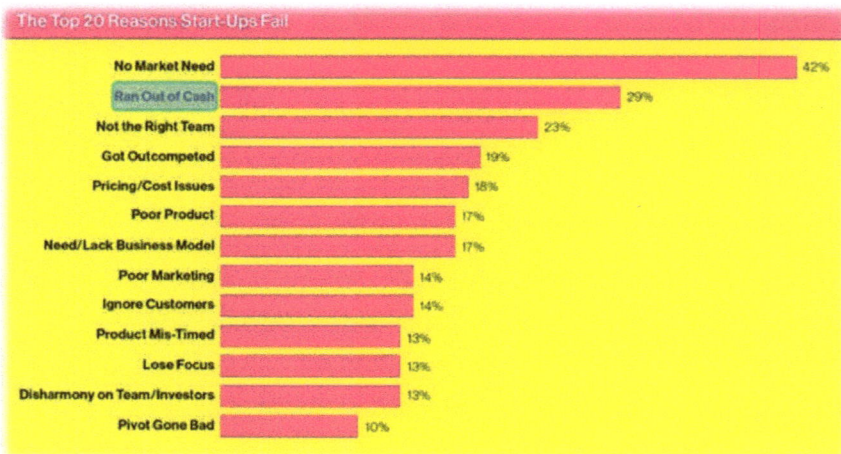

The Top 20 Reasons Start-Ups Fail	
No Market Need	42%
Ran Out of Cash	29%
Not the Right Team	23%
Got Outcompeted	19%
Pricing/Cost Issues	18%
Poor Product	17%
Need/Lack Business Model	17%
Poor Marketing	14%
Ignore Customers	14%
Product Mis-Timed	13%
Lose Focus	13%
Disharmony on Team/Investors	13%
Pivot Gone Bad	10%

Bringing Big Ideas to Life, Charles Plant (2)

In this chapter, we introduced some of the challenges that can hinder small and medium size businesses, and why some of these challenges must be addressed in a more critical way than corporate giants.

References

(1) Innovation, Science and Economic Development Canada, Key Small Business Statistics

(2) *Bringing Big Ideas to Life, Charles Plant,*
https://www.rotman.utoronto.ca/

Chapter 4 – Achieving Excellence Roadmap

Let us start with some poetry, an extract from The Road Not Taken by Robert Frost.

Two roads diverged in a wood, and I—I took the one less traveled by, And that has made all the difference.

We wish to point out the conundrum that is at hand. On the one hand, we need to follow our business strategy and aspirations, while on the other hand, we wish to ensure the success of our endeavours. Where do we start?

Too Many Roads to Get to Rome

Let us review some models to get an understanding of where we are heading.

First, Lean Principles come from Toyota and Taiichi Ohno. These principles provide a guideline in terms of what should be done step-by-step to increase the maturity of processes and deliveries in an organization.

I.   Define and focus on the **Value** as seen by the customer
     (reduce the waste)
II. Define and understand the **Value Stream**
     (design and improve the process, including setup time reduction, create understanding of the process)
III. Determine and optimize the **Flow**
     (understand takt time and its fluctuations, work to takt time and reduce batches, WIP)
IV. Ensure that the deliverables are **Pulled**
     (Kanban aka Just in Time)
V.   Aim for **Perfection**
     (continue to improve, reducing waste and variation)

Lean Principles (1)

The second model, proposed by John Kotter, focuses on Change Management and ensuring that necessary changes are effectively implemented and sustained within the organization. An interesting point about this model is the necessity of understanding the resistance to change rather than solely trying to reduce it. This deeper understanding can bring better and more adapted solutions.

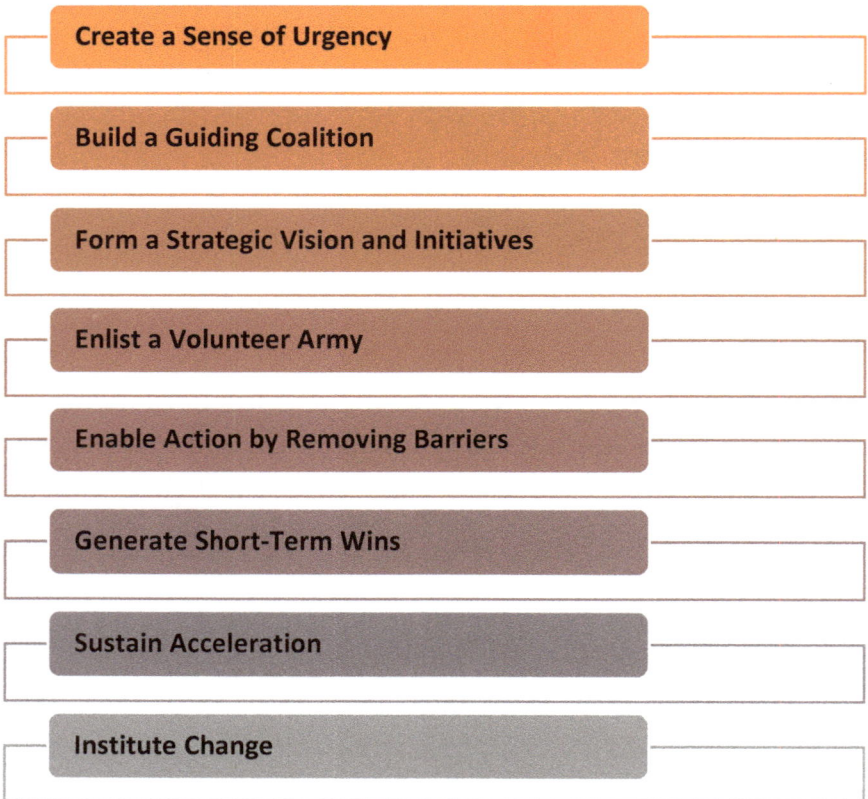

Create a Sense of Urgency

Build a Guiding Coalition

Form a Strategic Vision and Initiatives

Enlist a Volunteer Army

Enable Action by Removing Barriers

Generate Short-Term Wins

Sustain Acceleration

Institute Change

John Kotter, Change Management (2)

The third model is related to Business Process Management and was developed by Mike Hammer. This model emphasizes the importance of thoroughly identifying and clarifying all aspects of the key processes within a specific business.

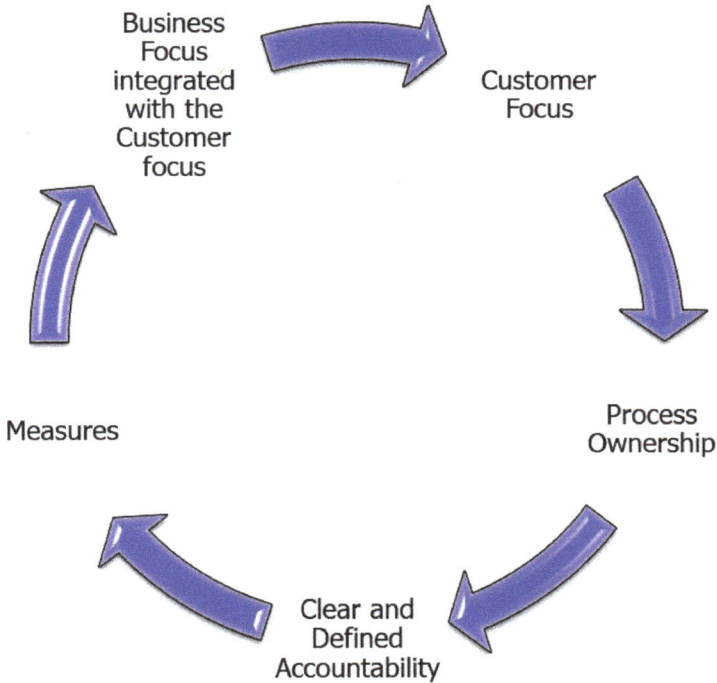

Mike Hammer, Business Process Management (3)

These models have been applied by thousands of corporations with varying degrees of success and sustainability. There are multiple aspects to consider — from the people involved, the business outcomes, and, of course, customer satisfaction.

The Achieving Excellence Roadmap discussed in this chapter combines these models and clarifies the action plan. It is an effort to consolidate numerous emerging best practices along with the three introduced models into a single methodology.

The Achieving Excellence Roadmap

Two roads diverged in a wood, and I—I took the action-driven one,
And that has made all the difference (Author unknown)

The road map consists of different columns that will be explained in more detail in the following chapters, along with many examples.

Focus on the Value Delivered to the Customer

This phase prioritizes customers and employees, ensuring that quick wins and improvements are achieved by actively involving them and fostering a strong foundation for engagement and culture. Strengthening leadership is also crucial as it forms an integral part of the solid base that must be established.

Understand and Define the Value Streams

We then develop a deep understanding of the key practices in the business and collaboratively examine the ways of working. How often do employees start to work in an environment where nothing is documented, and the only training they get is "watch me"? These practices need to be documented first and then improved.

Design and Innovate

This phase aims to elevate the consistency of experience and satisfaction for both employees and customers to a higher level. Some aspects of the ways of working will require a complete reimagining, encompassing processes, roles, responsibilities, and the technologies utilized.

Optimize the flow

Next comes optimization, focusing on enhancing performance and achieving excellence to become leaders in the field. This entails understanding demand and its fluctuations and having the capacity to model and refine processes accordingly.

Become Demand Focused

This phase enables growth by understanding the nuances of every request and the personalization and customization required by your customers. To use the motto from the Royal Canadian Logistics Service, "nemo secundus venit" which means "no one comes second"! Ensure that every single customer is taken care of, and consequently, every single employee.

References

(1) Lean Thinking, James Womack
(2) Leading Changes, John Kotter
(3) Reengineering The Corporation, Michael Hammer

Achieving Excellence Roadmap

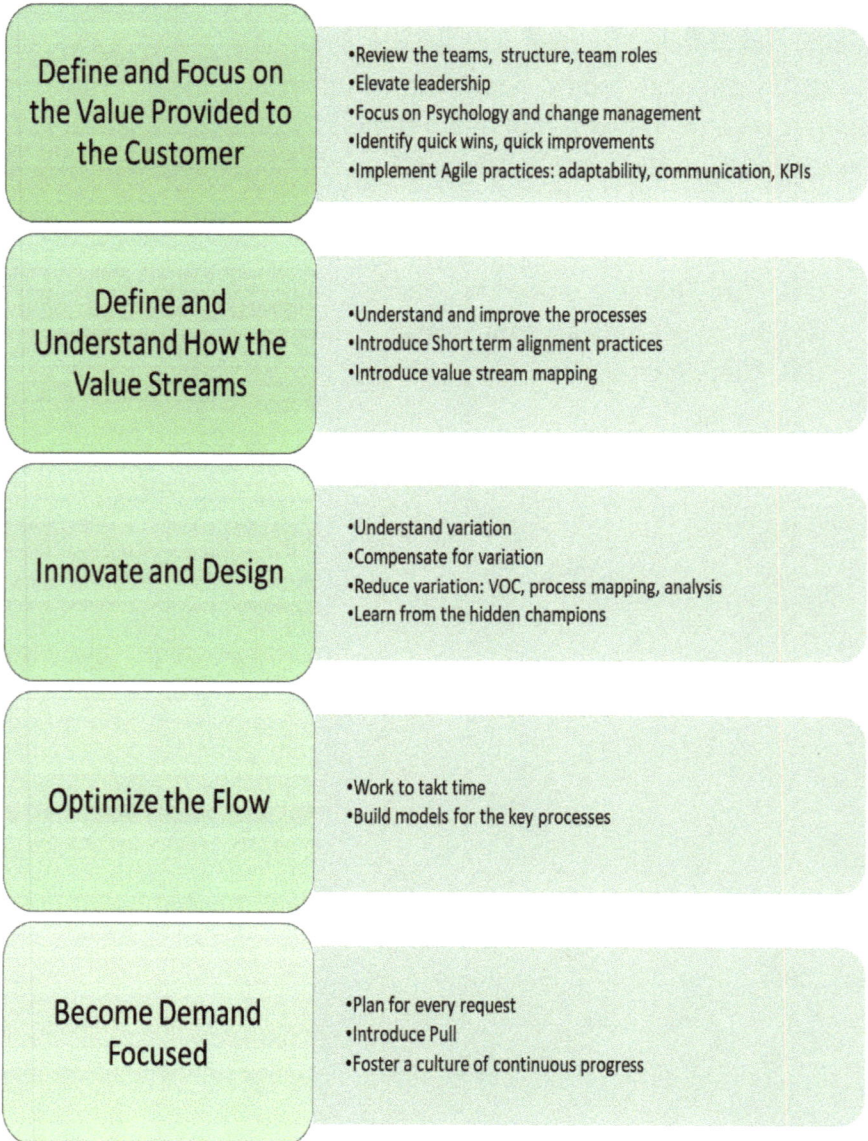

Define and Focus on the Value Provided to the Customer

- Review the teams, structure, team roles
- Elevate leadership
- Focus on Psychology and change management
- Identify quick wins, quick improvements
- Implement Agile practices: adaptability, communication, KPIs

Define and Understand How the Value Streams

- Understand and improve the processes
- Introduce Short term alignment practices
- Introduce value stream mapping

Innovate and Design

- Understand variation
- Compensate for variation
- Reduce variation: VOC, process mapping, analysis
- Learn from the hidden champions

Optimize the Flow

- Work to takt time
- Build models for the key processes

Become Demand Focused

- Plan for every request
- Introduce Pull
- Foster a culture of continuous progress

Total People Involvement   Voice of the Customer, Employees, Partners

33

Chapter 5 – An Overview of Business Fundamentals

Although this is not meant to be an MBA reference guide, it is important to review and understand some key business fundamentals. The following chapter presents reflection points and several hints for assessing the condition of your business.

What about Our Market?

Which market strategy are we adopting to grow our market: growing deep or growing wide?

Growing wide involves expanding the customer base and reaching new markets. This can be achieved through tactics such as increasing brand awareness, launching new products, or entering new geographic locations. The most frequent tactic is to focus on low-cost services and low-cost products. We can easily think about low-cost online classes related to Lean Six Sigma. For example, a Greenbelt training could be completed by spending $100. The training may be of good quality, but it may lack distinctive learning elements or exclusive features.

On the other hand, growing deeply involves increasing sales and loyalty within the existing customer base. This can be achieved through tactics such as upselling, cross-selling, or improving customer retention. Smartphones such as iPhones or Samsung are a great example of these.

Low Price Wide Market	Low Price Narrow Market
High Product Grade Wide Market	High Product Grade Narrow Market

Growth

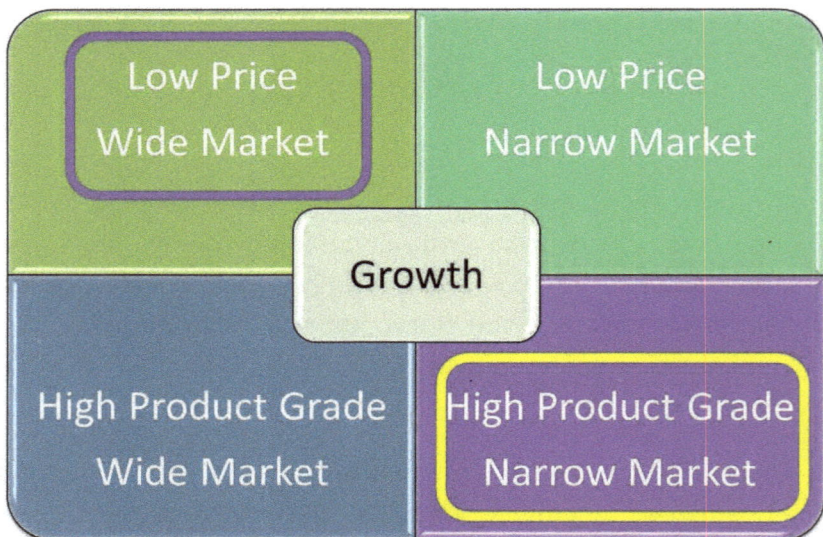

Marketing Strategy

Ultimately, the choice between growing wide or deep will depend on factors such as the business's goals and resources, as well as the conditions of the market. It is important to carefully evaluate these factors before deciding on a growth strategy, as it will impact the type of staffing, organizational set-up, and pricing structure.

Where are the market opportunities?

Furthermore, to understand which strategy to adopt, it is important to understand the market size and the opportunities that we are facing. The Boston Consulting Group matrix is one way to visualize where our products and services are located. Here is an overview of the four quadrants, along with the typical recommended strategies.

-   Stars: These are products with high market share in a high-growth market. They have the potential to generate significant profits but may require investment to maintain their position.

- Cash Cows: These are products with high market share in a low-growth market. They generate steady profits and require little investment.
- Question Marks: These are products with low market share in a high-growth market. They have the potential for growth but may require significant investment to increase their market share.
- Dogs: These are products with a low market share in a low-growth market. They generate low profits and may be candidates for divestment.

Let us keep in mind that these are all recommendations, and as a business, we might decide to pursue other avenues. For example, General Electric decided to invest in its dogs in the 1990s. By selling GE Appliances at a higher price, the business went from a worth of 4 billion USD to being sold for 5.4 billion USD!

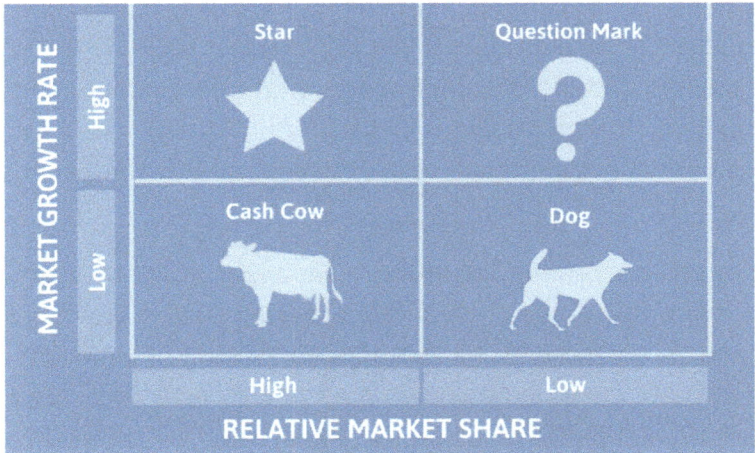

Boston Consulting Group Matrix (1)

Deciding on our marketing mix

The marketing 4 C's are a modern take on the traditional marketing mix, 4 P's, which includes product, price, place, and promotion. The 4 C's, on the other hand, focus on the customer and include customer needs and wants, cost to the customer, convenience, and communication. This approach emphasizes the importance of understanding the customer's perspective, creating a marketing strategy that meets their needs and desires, and securing an optimal volume of leads.

Monitoring customer satisfaction and loyalty.

Customer Satisfaction Score **(CSAT)** and Net Promoter Score **(NPS)** are two popular metrics used to measure customer satisfaction and loyalty. Both are needed!

CSAT measures a customer's satisfaction with a specific interaction or experience, such as a purchase or customer service interaction. It is typically measured using a survey that asks customers to rate their satisfaction on a scale such as 1-5 or 1-10. It is more rational to evaluate the experience and satisfaction with the product or service.

NPS, on the other hand, measures a customer's overall loyalty to a brand or company. It is calculated by asking customers how likely they are to recommend the company to a friend or colleague on a scale of 0-10. Customers who give a score of 9-10 are considered promoters, while those who give a score of 0-6 are considered detractors. The NPS is calculated by subtracting the percentage of detractors from the percentage of promoters. NPS is about emotions and how much we would promote a brand or company.

In summary, CSAT measures satisfaction with a specific interaction, while NPS measures overall loyalty to a brand or company. While we may give a perfect score of 10 out of 10 in terms of the CSAT, our excitement about the product may only warrant a 7, leading us to withhold promotion. Take the example of Polysporin or a car oil change. High satisfaction would result from a prompt bruise healing or a quick and efficient oil change, meaning that the CSAT would be high. Nevertheless, these experiences would not be shared with our close friends or colleagues as they do not result in much excitement.

Net Promoter Score

Cash is King

Cash and working capital are crucial for the smooth operation of a business. **Cash** is the lifeblood of a business, allowing it to pay its bills, invest in growth, and weather unexpected challenges. **Working capital**, on the other hand, is the difference between a company's current assets and current liabilities. Without a doubt, cash is a key component of working capital. Working capital represents the funds available to a business to finance its day-to-day operations. A healthy level of working capital is essential for a business to meet its short-term obligations, such as paying suppliers, employees, and creditors. Without sufficient cash and working capital, a business may struggle to operate effectively and may even face bankruptcy.

A very simple way to calculate working capital is to estimate the **days of working capital**, which is how many days it takes for a company to convert its working capital into revenue. The lower, the better!

The calculations are explained below, and all you need are your financial statements. A comparison of Apple vs Boeing is used. Although comparing these companies is like comparing pears to papaya, it highlights the working capital advantage of Apple (-40 days).

$$D_{\text{Working Capital}} = D_{\text{Inventory}} + D_{\text{Receivables}} - D_{\text{Payable}}$$

Days of Inventory = (inventory /annual COGS) *365

Days of receivables = (AR / annual sales) *365

Days of payables = (AP / annual COGS) * 365

Boeing - values in 000's (FY end on Dec 31, 2022)		2022
Sales	$	66,608,000
Cost of Sales	$	63,106,000
Receivables (unbilled for LT contracts would add 8,620)	$	11,305,000
Payables	$	31,781,000
Inventory	$	78,151,000

Apple - values in 000's (FY end on Sept 25, 2022)		2022
Sales	$	394,328,000
Cost of Sales	$	223,546,000
Receivables	$	60,932,000
Payables	$	64,115,000
Inventory	$	4,946,000

Boeing	
DI	452
DR	62
DP	184
DWC	330

Apple	
DI	8
DR	56
DP	105
DWC	- 40

Days of Working Capital Examples

Here are a few red flags to keep in mind if you are wondering how good your cash situation is.

- Operating with less than three times your monthly expenditures available as cash in the bank.

- More than half of your receivables are unpaid 90 days after the date of the invoice.
- Some long-term clients started to pay you more slowly but they are ordering more or are requesting an extension for their invoices.
- You have been in business for more than five years, and your operating expenses routinely eclipse your gross sales.
- You are very reliant on your line of credit.
- There is no communication between the Sales and Finance departments.

What about profit?

Well, we may not be profitable yet maintain a strong cash position, similar to Uber. Thus, cash comes in first.

Let's talk about profit, Baby.

Profit is the financial gain that a business makes after deducting all expenses. It is an important measure of a company's financial health and success. There are several ways to measure profit, including gross profit, operating profit, and net profit.

Gross profit is calculated by subtracting the cost of goods sold from revenue. It represents the profit a company makes after accounting for the direct costs of producing its goods or services.

Operating profit is calculated by subtracting operating expenses from gross profit. It represents the profit a company makes from its core business operations before accounting for interest and taxes.

Net profit is calculated by subtracting all expenses, including interest and taxes, from revenue. It represents the profit a company makes after accounting for all expenses.

Each of these measures provides a different perspective on a company's profitability and can be useful for evaluating its financial performance.

Although net profit presents a comprehensive measure of profitability, we typically rely on gross profit and operating profit in the short term due to their simpler calculation and ongoing monitoring.

Business solvency

Business solvency ratios are financial metrics used to measure a company's ability to meet its long-term obligations. These ratios provide insight into the financial health and stability of a company and are often used by investors, creditors, and analysts to assess the risk associated with lending to or investing in a company.

Some common solvency ratios include the debt-to-equity ratio, which measures the proportion of a company's funding that comes from debt relative to equity and the cash flow test, which measures a company's ability to meet its interest payments on outstanding debt.

Cash Flow Test: Can the business pay its debts when payments become due? If your business cannot pay expenses, employees, creditors, or Income Tax, then the business could be insolvent.

Solvency Ratio or Debt-to-Equity Ratio:

$$\frac{Debt}{Equity} = \frac{Total\ Equity}{Total\ Liabilities}$$

Depending on the type of industry, there are different benchmarks to determine how good or how bad a particular ratio is. Generally, a good debt-to-equity ratio is anything lower than 1.0. A ratio of between 1 and 1.5 is considered 'good' as it might suggest that debt is being used to finance business growth. A ratio of 2.0 or higher is usually considered risky.

Final Considerations

In this chapter, we discussed a few business fundamentals, mostly related to the market and financial considerations. These are the primary aspects that always need to be assessed and addressed first. Other factors can also be assessed, such as skills available in the organization, the management team competencies, and capabilities within the organization.

An inventory of skills available and skills missing helps plan and understand what future requests the customers would bring and if the organization can meet demands for these requests. If there are gaps, talent development and hiring can be considered when the opportunities are worth it.

Management competencies can change the game in terms of customer approach, team coaching, team management, and development. Let us refer to this picture that was introduced and explained in Chapter 1.

The organizational capabilities refer to the products and services that we can take on in terms of volume, expertise, risk level, and risk appetite.

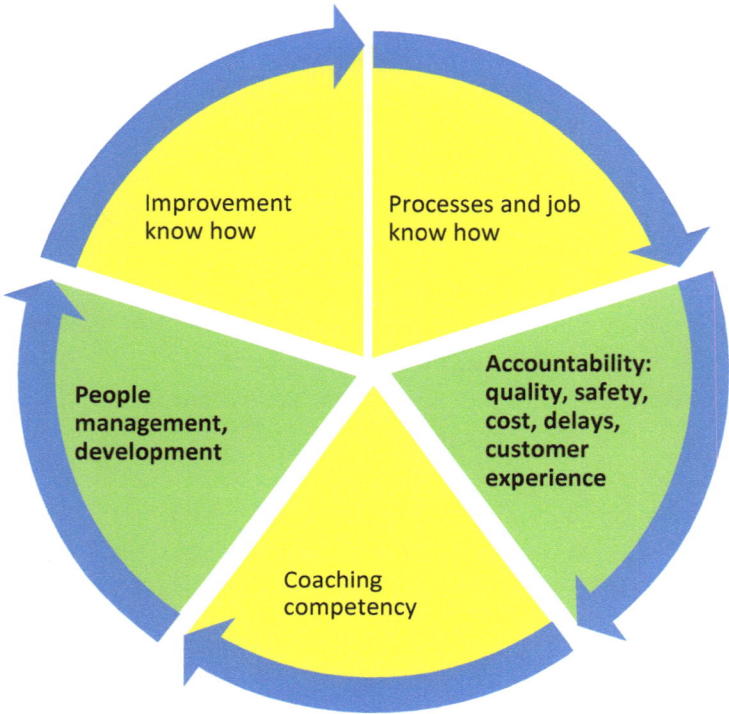

Management competencies

References

(1) https://www.bcg.com/about/overview/our-history/growth-share-matrix

Chapter 6 – Define and Focus on the Value Provided to the Customer

Define and Focus on the Value Provided to the Customer

- Review the teams, structure, team roles
- Elevate leadership
- Focus on Psychology and change management
- Identify quick wins, quick improvements
- Implement Agile practices: adaptability, communication, KPIs

This first step is to put customers and employees first to ensure that the quick wins and improvements are achieved by involving them and creating a strong foundation for engagement and culture. Leadership also needs to be strengthened as it is part of the solid base that needs to be established.

The teams and Structure

A team's energy and empowerment are essential for any organization. In Chapter 2, we saw different methods on how to motivate people and create a suitable environment for it.

One basic idea is that employees should not be seen as subordinates, but as partners in entrepreneurship. Being able to experiment and deliver results provides a great sense of achievement. For instance, when I worked as an engineer at General Electric, I oversaw launching new designs, from idea to production. I felt like a mini entrepreneur, but I also had a team of seniors and juniors, and many others to consult. I was mentored and coached along the way, and I sought advice and help from others. Hierarchy did not exist here.

Another factor for making a collaborative and empowering work culture is the organizational structure. Traditional hierarchical structures can create rigid limits and silos between departments and levels, which can affect communication, innovation, and autonomy. Flat organizational structures, on the other hand, try to reduce or eliminate unnecessary levels of management and bureaucracy, and promote a culture of collaboration and trust among team members. Flat organizations can have several benefits over non-flat ones, such as:

- Faster decision-making and problem-solving, as team members can communicate directly with each other and do not have to wait for approval from multiple managers.

- Higher employee engagement and satisfaction, as team members feel more valued and respected for their contributions and ideas and have more opportunities to gain experience and grow.

- Greater flexibility and agility, as team members can adapt quickly to changing customer needs and market conditions, and experiment with new approaches and solutions.

- Lower costs and overhead, as flat organizations can operate more efficiently and effectively with fewer resources and less waste.

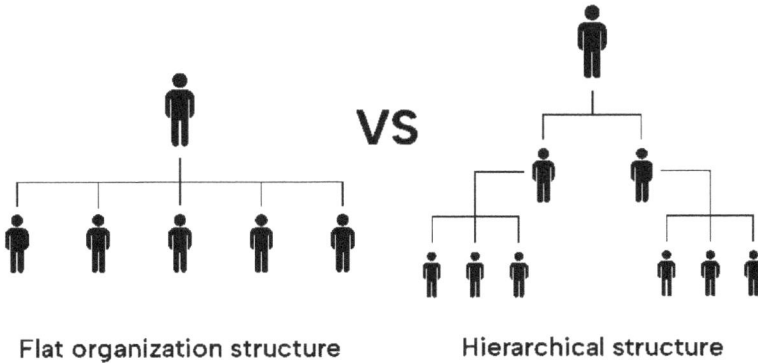

Flat organization structure   Hierarchical structure

Flat structure vs hierarchical structure

However, flat organizational structures are not perfect!

Here are some points to also consider:

The lack of clarity and coordination, as team members may not have clear roles and responsibilities and may encounter conflicts or confusion over priorities and expectations. Frequent touchpoints and communications are needed to ensure clarity. This is where the mentoring and coaching part becomes extremely useful, in addition to frequent huddles.

In larger organizations, the flat concept is reproduced by having a matrix structure, where each lead collaborates with individuals from different functions, without daily involvement from individual managers.

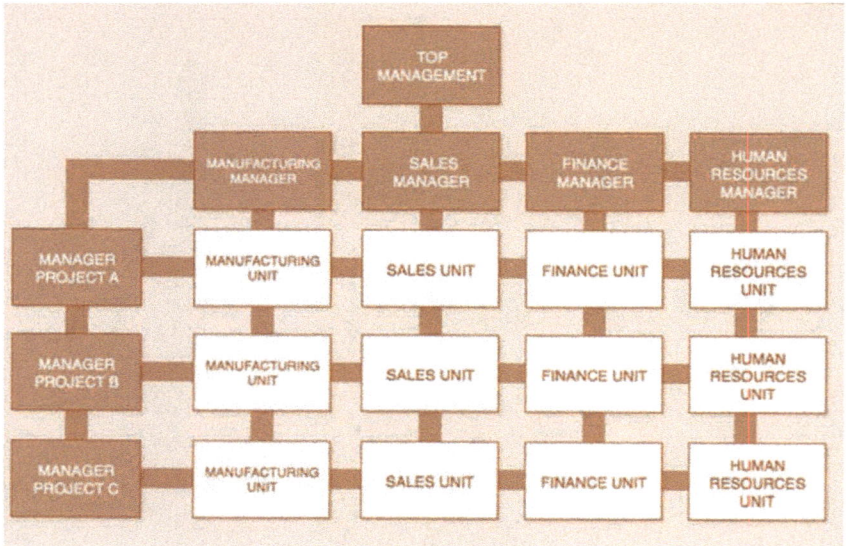

Matrix Structure

Leadership

At this stage, an evaluation of the manager's leadership style is necessary. For example, assessing how much impact and influence a manager has and if team members reach out to them for coaching or mentoring are important metrics.

Key training should be offered to these managers, such as listening skills, coaching (giving feedback), and situational leadership.

Listening, coaching, and giving feedback go hand in hand. These skills are interrelated and can be applied in different situations depending on the needs and preferences of the employees.

Active listening is the ability to pay attention to what others are saying, both verbally and non-verbally, and to understand their perspective, emotions, and concerns. Listening helps managers build rapport and trust with their employees, as well as identify their strengths, weaknesses, and areas of improvement. Listening also enables managers to recognize and address any issues or conflicts that may arise among the team members or with other stakeholders.

Giving feedback is the act of sharing specific, timely, and actionable information about the employees' performance, behaviour, or attitude, to reinforce what they are doing well, correct what they are doing wrong, and encourage them to improve and grow. Giving feedback helps managers motivate and appreciate their employees, as well as address any gaps or challenges that may hinder their progress or potential. Giving feedback also helps managers monitor and evaluate the employees' results and outcomes, as well as ensure accountability and quality standards.

Coaching is the process of guiding and supporting employees in their learning and development, by asking open-ended questions, providing constructive feedback, and offering resources and opportunities. Coaching helps managers empower their employees to take ownership of their performance, goals, and career path, as well as enhance their skills, knowledge, and confidence. Coaching also helps managers align the employees' individual objectives with the team's and the organization's vision and strategy.

Psychology - Situational Leadership

Situational leadership (1) is the ability to adjust one's leadership style and approach according to the needs, preferences, and readiness of the employees and the situation. Situational leadership helps managers adopt the most effective and appropriate way of communicating, delegating, motivating, and supporting their employees, depending on the level of competence and commitment they demonstrate for a specific task or goal. Situational leadership also helps managers foster flexibility and adaptability among their employees, as well as respond to the changing demands and challenges of the environment.

The core concept of situational leadership is that there is not one best way to lead but rather a continuum of leadership styles that can be applied in different circumstances. The situational leadership model, developed by Paul Hersey and Ken Blanchard, identifies four main leadership styles: directing, coaching, supporting, and delegating. Each style corresponds to a different combination of task-oriented and relationship-oriented behaviours, as shown in the table below.

Style	Directive Behavior	Support Behavior
Directing	High	Low
Coaching	High	High
Supporting	Low	High
Delegating	Low	Low

The situational leadership model also suggests that the leadership style should match the development level of the employee for a given task or goal. The development level is determined by the employee's competence (knowledge and skills) and commitment (motivation and confidence) to the task or goal. The model identifies four main development levels: enthusiastic beginner, disillusioned learner, capable but cautious performer, and self-reliant achiever. Each level corresponds to a different degree of readiness and willingness to perform the task or goal, as shown in the table below.

Level	Competence With the task	Commitment	Readiness
Enthusiastic Beginner	Low	High	R1
Disillusioned Learner	Low	Low	R2
Capable but Cautious Performer	High	Low	R3
Self-Reliant Achiever	High	High	R4

- For employees who are enthusiastic beginners (R1), the directing style (S1) is most effective, as it provides clear instructions, expectations, and feedback, as well as close supervision and guidance. Typical examples are employees who just joined the company or who were transferred to a new function or a new project. Someone who is an enthusiastic beginner could have 20 years of experience, still beginning in a new role.

- For employees who are disillusioned learners (R2), the coaching style (S2) is most effective, as it provides both high direction and high support, as well as encouragement, involvement, and explanation. There are typically people who realise that the grass is not as green as they thought and need more support to get through that phase.

- For employees who are capable but cautious performers (R3), the supporting style (S3) is most effective, as it provides low direction and high support, as well as praise, recognition, and collaboration. Many employees would relate to this profile, working competently while juggling work and personal concerns at home.

- For employees who are self-reliant achievers (R4), the delegating style (S4) is most effective, as it provides low direction and low support, as well as autonomy, responsibility, and trust. These are the people that you typically see reading articles or registering to webinars during their lunch breaks. We are all achievers on certain tasks that we perform. Have you ever felt micromanaged? These were some situations where you were an achiever and you felt that someone was breathing down your neck!

This situational leadership model allows managers to learn to adapt their approach and would allow them to get much more respect and acknowledgement from their employees.

Another part of psychology is related to frequent communication through huddles, and this concept is described further down in the agile section.

Identify Quick Wins, Quick Improvements

A common hurdle in any type of turnaround or improvement situation is to try to do everything at the same time. We are trying to eat the elephant all at once, and as the expression says, we need to eat the elephant one bite at a time. Please note that I love elephants!

A useful tool for managers who want to improve their situation or achieve their goals is the **SWOT analysis**. SWOT stands for Strengths, Weaknesses, Opportunities, and Threats. It is a simple but powerful framework that helps to identify the internal and external factors that affect the performance of an organization, project, or individual.

Strengths	Weaknesses
• What advantages do you have? • What do you do well? • What relevant resources do you have access to? • What do other people see as your strengths? • In looking at your strengths, think about them in relation to your competitors	• What could you improve? • What do you do badly? • What should you avoid?
Opportunities	**Threats**
• Where are the good opportunities facing you? • What are the interesting trends you are aware of? • Look at your strengths and ask yourself whether these open up any opportunities. Alternatively, look at your weaknesses and ask yourself whether you could open up opportunities by eliminating them.	• What obstacles do you face? • What is your competition doing? • Are the required specifications for your job, products or services changing? • Is changing technology threatening our position? • Could any of your weaknesses seriously threaten our business?

SWOT Analysis

To use the SWOT analysis, gather some of your team members and start to list the strengths and weaknesses of your current situation, as well as the opportunities and threats that exist in the environment. Strengths are the positive attributes or advantages that one has, such as skills, resources, reputation, or loyal customers. Weaknesses are the negative aspects or limitations that one faces, such as gaps, inefficiencies, costs, or risks. Opportunities are the favourable situations or trends that one can exploit, such as new markets, technologies, partnerships, or regulations. Threats are unfavourable situations or trends that one needs to overcome, such as competition, changes, disruptions, or obstacles.

Having in hand a few of the business fundamentals assessments discussed in the previous chapter can be quite handy. For example, we can link with customer feedback such as praises or complaints. As the SWOT is being filled, interviews with employees or customers and meetings with small groups, which we refer to as focus groups, are also quick ways to get the information that we need. This would also help us understand what the real value is and the needs of the customers that require our focus.

The SWOT analysis can help managers identify the key issues and priorities that they need to address, as well as potential strategies and actions that they can take. For example, by matching the strengths and opportunities, one can find ways to leverage the existing assets and capabilities to seize new opportunities. By matching the weaknesses and threats, one can find ways to minimize the impact or eliminate the sources of vulnerability and danger. By matching the strengths and threats, one can find ways to defend the position and counter the challenges. By matching the weaknesses and opportunities, one can find ways to improve the situation and overcome the barriers.

You will find below an example related to social services that we worked on. There are a lot of elements, and once this SWOT analysis is developed, we will vote on the items that we wish to address first. Voting can seem challenging, as gathering extensive data to make informed decisions is ideal. However, attempting to collect data on everything can lead to analysis paralysis. Pragmatically speaking, we vote first, and then we gather information about what we voted on.

Strengths	Weaknesses
Interdisciplinary team	Delays and long wait times to obtain services
Skilled and trained professionals abiding by Code of Ethics	Hierarchical structure and slow in implementing changes due to the bureaucratic process
Government funding	Standardization and regulation leading to an increase in paperwork, standardized assessments, and rigid protocols
Partnerships and relationships with various community organizations and agencies	Gaps in services for marginalized populations (e.g. unhoused, refugees, etc.)
Providing free and essential services and resources to public	Limited resources and funding
Integrated services	Employee burnout
Variety of services for various populations	Understaffed and staff turnover
Positive impact on individuals and communities	Limited avenues to create awareness about offerings and programs to the general public

Opportunities	Threats
Optimization of technology (e.g., digitization of client files)	Privatization - quicker services for clients
Increased government funding and support through awareness of demand	Privatization - enhanced remuneration for employees resulting in losing employees
Promote EDIA	Use of technology leading to employees' perception of being monitored
Increase in awareness and education leading to a reduction in social stigma	Shift in supervision from a learning environment to implementing cheques and balances
Societal demand for support post COVID-19 (e.g., mental health, resources)	Changes in forms of government and budget for social services
Various services to encompass Canada's diverse population	Difficulty navigating the system (e.g., first point of contact, referral process, eligibility criteria)
Collaboration with private sector, community organizations, and agencies	Escalating demand for social services due to growing disparities
Offer expanded value added programs with extra funding or a fee	Aging population leading to demand for services tailored to older adults and increased needs necessitating enhanced fund
Funding for palliative care (demand on the rise)	Labour shortage

SWOT Analysis – Social Services

Once decisions are made from the SWOT analysis, we can then focus on reducing the non-value-added activities and enhancing the value-added ones. But what does value-added mean?

Quick Wins – MUDA

Value added is a term that refers to any activity or process that increases the quality, usefulness, or desirability of a product or service for the customer! Think about grocery shopping; there are multiple activities that we need to perform, but what we wish is a quick service and low cost, as well as great and fresh food. Value-added activities are essential for creating value and satisfying customer needs and expectations.

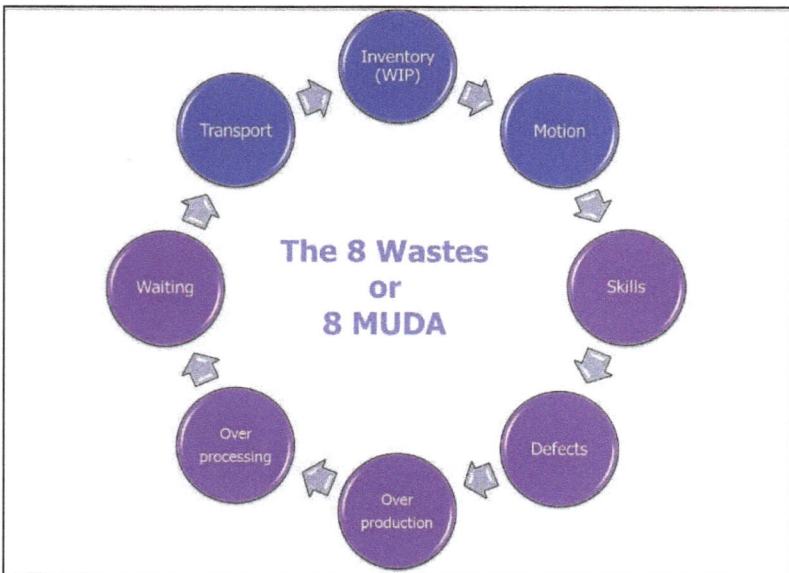

The eight wastes, organized around the TIMWOODS acronym

Non-value added, on the other hand, is a term that refers to any activity or process that consumes resources but does not add any value to the product or service from the customer's perspective. Non-value-added activities are considered wasteful and should be eliminated or minimized as much as possible. Again, in the grocery shopping experience discussed above, consider the wasted time spent searching for items, selecting fresh products over those that are not, and waiting in line.

Non-value-added activities are also referred to as wastes, or in Japanese, by the word MUDA. Why use Japanese? It is much easier to say to anyone that we need to work on MUDA and that what we are doing daily is MUDA then saying to people that what we have been doing is non-value added, which sounds very condescending.

The first step in terms of eliminating MUDA is to identify it. MUDA encompasses eight types of wastes that can occur in any process: defects, overproduction, waiting, transportation, inventory, motion, overprocessing, and skills. By eliminating or reducing these wastes, the process can become more efficient, quick, cheap, and provide value added. It is possible to help people in a grocery store find the items quicker. We can also position the most popular items in a way that customers create a more pleasant shopping experience. We can also reduce waiting times.

Let us take a closer look at each of the eight wastes of lean and how they can affect different sectors:

Transportation: This is the waste of unnecessary movement or handling of products or materials. Transportation increases the risk of damage, loss, or deterioration. It also adds time and cost to the process. For example, transportation could be moving goods from one warehouse to another, transferring files from one department to another, or transporting patients from one ward to another.

Inventory: This is the waste of excess stock or supplies that are not being used or processed. Inventory ties up capital, space, and resources. It also hides quality problems and demand fluctuations. For example, inventory could be a pile of unsold clothes, a stack of unused paper, or a surplus of medication.

Motion: This is the waste of unnecessary movement or actions by people or machines. Motion causes fatigue, injury, wear and tear, and inefficiency. For example, motion could be walking back and forth to fetch tools, bending or reaching to perform a task, or adjusting a machine setting.

Waiting: This is the waste of idle time when people, machines, or materials are not ready or available. Waiting reduces productivity, efficiency, and flow. For example, waiting could be a long queue at a checkout counter, a machine breakdown, or a delay in getting test results.

Overproduction: This is the waste of producing more than what is needed or producing it too early. Overproduction leads to excess inventory, storage costs, spoilage, and obsolescence. For example, overproduction could be making too many pizzas, printing too many brochures, or ordering too many tests for a patient.

Overprocessing: This is the waste of doing more work or adding more features than what is required or valued by the customer. Overprocessing consumes extra time, energy, and materials. It also increases complexity and variability. For example, overprocessing could be polishing a product that will be painted, adding extra toppings to a pizza, or performing unnecessary procedures on a patient.

Defects: These are the errors or mistakes that result in poor-quality products or services that do not meet customer expectations. Defects cause rework, scrap, returns, complaints, and loss of reputation. For example, defects could be a faulty car part, a wrong order in a restaurant, or a misdiagnosis in a hospital.

Skills: This is the waste of underutilizing or ignoring the talents, abilities, and ideas of people. Skills waste lowers morale, motivation, and creativity. It also leads to high turnover, low performance, and missed opportunities. For example, skills waste could be assigning a skilled worker to a mundane task, not listening to employee feedback, or not providing adequate training or development.

Identifying the wastes can bring ideas right away. As an example, in an emergency department where we were involved, nurses and doctors were spending hours each day looking for different sizes of gloves, patient files, and gowns. The typical patient would wait about half an hour as these key items were being retrieved before proceeding to an exam. Once we identified the wastes, which consisted of motion and waiting, we were able to reduce that wait time to 6 minutes.

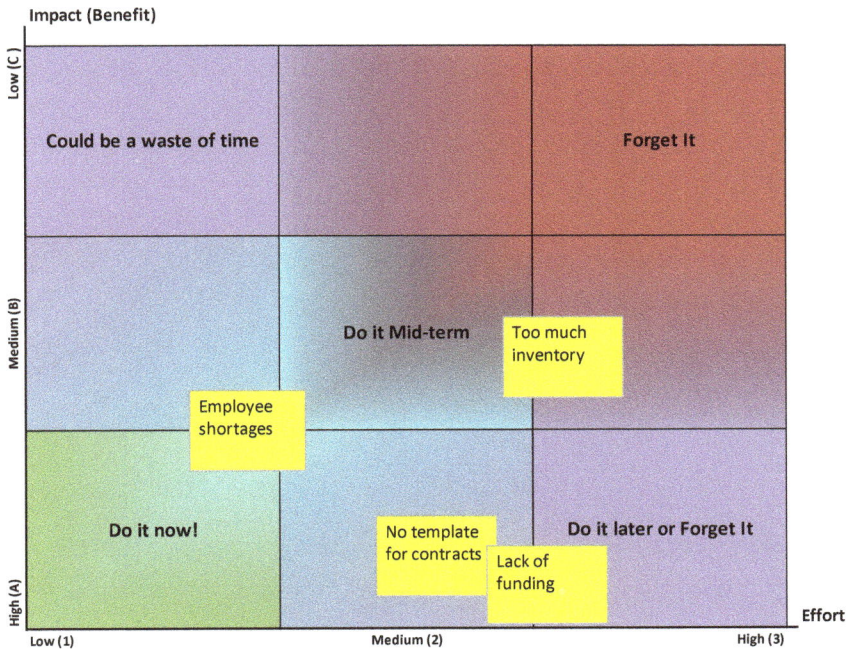

Benefit vs effort matrix

Quick Wins - Benefit vs Effort Matrix

If there are too many items that need to be considered or too many problems or activities, the Benefit versus Effort Matrix can be used to help make a choice.

In the example below, which comes from a company that offers information technology services, we would start with the low effort and high benefit as a priority. As we get further from the Green Zone, the activities become either more difficult or less relevant. Keep in mind that the matrix does not decide for you! It is a guideline, and you can still decide to pursue any activity that has been listed.

Quick Wins - Bureaucracy and SCAMPER

SCAMPER is a creative thinking tool that was developed by Alex Osborn, the father of brainstorming, to stimulate and expand the thinking process. It is based on the idea that new ideas or solutions can be generated by applying different types of transformations to an existing problem or product. The acronym stands for:

- Substitute: replace one element with another

- Combine: merge two or more elements together

- Adapt: modify an element to suit a new purpose or context

- Modify: change an element in some way, such as size, shape, colour, or purpose.

- Put to another use: find a new application or function for an element

- Eliminate: remove an unnecessary or redundant element

- Reverse: invert or rearrange the order or direction of an element, search as asking suppliers for a performance report instead of providing a performance report to suppliers.

An element can be a meeting, a report, software, a tool, or another.

One can use SCAMPER to cut down on red tape in organizations by questioning the current processes, rules, and structures that may be wasteful, old-fashioned, or blocking innovation. By using SCAMPER questions, such as "What can we replace to make this process easier?" or "What can we remove to decrease the number of approvals required?", one can find possible areas for enhancement and create different solutions that are more flexible, efficient, and adaptable to the evolving demands of the organization and its customers.

When I started working for General Electric, we had some SCAMPER afternoons once a month to reduce bureaucracy as part of our daily and weekly tasks.

Agile practices - Team Huddles or Stand-Ups

This part could have been written in the psychology section as it is pretty much related! Frequent huddles within a team in any organization or department is highly recommended. It fosters communication and collaboration among team members. What is a huddle? It is a short, focused meeting where team members share updates, challenges, feedback, and ideas. By having regular huddles, team members can stay informed, aligned, and engaged with each other and the project goals. Huddles can also help to resolve issues, identify opportunities, and celebrate successes.

Keep in mind that huddles are designed for collaboration, not for micromanagement or keeping track of what people are working on. If there are any issues with team members in terms of performance, these conversations should happen on a one-on-one basis outside of the huddle!

It is recommended to build an agenda before the huddle. Here is an example of a 10-minute huddle. Huddles can be made fun of by using some humour, passing a ball once it is one's turn to speak, or similar ideas.

a. Good news or bad news about what is happening around the team.
b. Review of very few performance indicators (maximum 3).
c. Round table to share updates and the daily priorities of everyone.
d. Any hurdle that team members would like to bring.
e. Joke of the day or of the week!

Let us keep in mind that it is OK for team members to not be happy with what is going on and share their problems. As Shigeo Shingo once said, dissatisfaction with the status quo brings forth the need for improvement and change.

To wrap up this section, we focused on the first steps to achieve some early wins and motivate our team members. We do not want to bite off more than what we can chew.

References

(1) Management of Organizational Behavior, Paul Hersey, Kenneth Blanchard

Achieving Excellence Roadmap

Define and Focus on the Value Provided to the Customer
- Review the teams, structure, team roles
- Elevate leadership
- Focus on Psychology and change management
- Identify quick wins, quick improvements
- Implement Agile practices: adaptability, communication, KPIs

Define and Understand How the Value Streams
- Understand and improve the processes
- Introduce Short term alignment practices
- Introduce value stream mapping

Innovate and Design
- Understand variation
- Compensate for variation
- Reduce variation: VOC, process mapping, analysis
- Learn from the hidden champions

Optimize the Flow
- Work to takt time
- Build models for the key processes

Become Demand Focused
- Plan for every request
- Introduce Pull
- Foster a culture of continuous progress

Total People Involvement Voice of the Customer, Employees, Partners

62

Chapter 7 – Define and Understand How the Value Streams

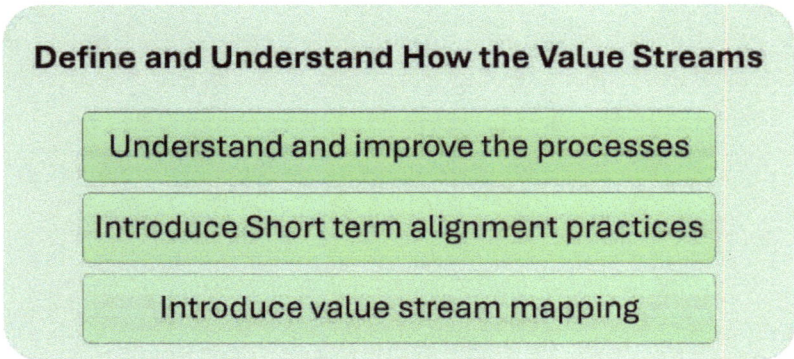

Define and Understand How the Value Streams

> Understand and improve the processes
>
> Introduce Short term alignment practices
>
> Introduce value stream mapping

The first step we took was to prioritize our customers and employees, focusing on the value we need to provide. We discussed quick wins to get everyone on board.

The second step in this journey consists of understanding how we manage the value from A to Z. We sometimes refer to this concept as the value chain. The value chain may consist of requests from our customers, bringing different types of inputs such as materials, information, and other types of resources, and then transforming these to create the required outputs or results. We need to understand exactly what steps are involved, or what we tend to call "high-level processes". Once we establish this understanding, we need to ensure that people comprehend these processes, monitor their performance and improve them if needed. This is the essence of a value stream map. The term 'value stream' evokes the image of water streaming effortlessly down a river. In a Barbie world or ideal world, the value would flow from A to Z without any constraint.

In this chapter, we will thoroughly cover the overall steps with many examples. In the next chapter, we will detail the improvement tools as well as value stream mapping.

The Value Chain and Core Processes

Core processes are the activities that directly contribute to creating and delivering value to customers and stakeholders. They are usually cross-functional and span multiple departments or divisions. For example, product development, marketing, sales, and customer service are core processes for a business that develops and sells computer servers.

Support processes are the activities that enable or facilitate the core processes. They do not directly create value for customers, but they are necessary for the efficient and effective functioning of the organization. Examples of support processes include human resources, finance, IT, procurement, health and safety, etc.

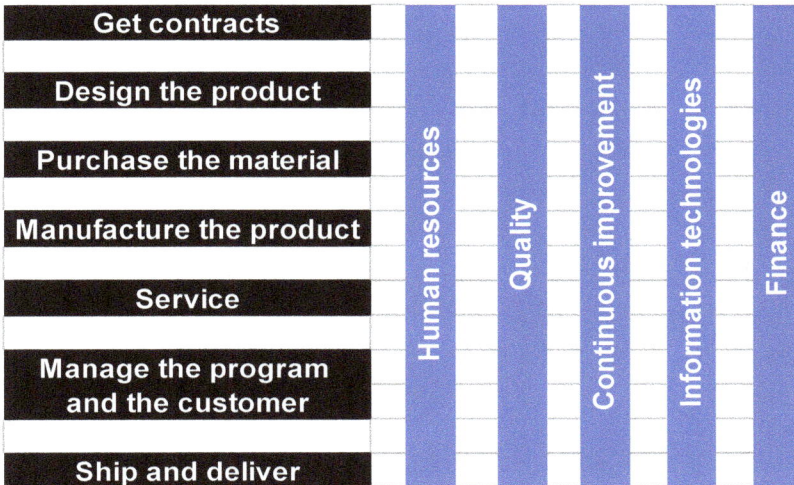

Get contracts					
Design the product	Human resources	Quality	Continuous improvement	Information technologies	Finance
Purchase the material					
Manufacture the product					
Service					
Manage the program and the customer					
Ship and deliver					

Core processes (Black horizontal) and Support processes (Blue vertical)

If we refer to the example above, the value chain is defined by the core process in black (horizontal). Delivering their value would be impossible without going through those processes. We need to keep in mind that without those represented in blue (horizontal), delivering the value would be extremely challenging! Thus, we need to start by establishing and documenting these ones first.

Create Understanding of the Processes

Once we establish that high level picture, we need to establish and document these core processes first. How many times have you started a new job and on the first day you were told "watch me and learn how we do things here!"? Although observation is a key aspect of learning, there needs to be a foundation that serves as a reference and standard for everyone. For example, we consulted in a medical software company where every sales manager had their own template to send a proposal to a client. This was very confusing for all the different departments working with sales, as well as for their customers, as they were never receiving the same information or format from project to project.

We need to document these processes in a way that is easy to understand, such as a procedure or a work instruction, sometimes referred to as a standard operating procedure (SOP). The document typically consists of a one-page summary of the process in the form of a process map, then a few pages with the necessary details and visuals such as pictures and screenshots. It is recommended to avoid 50-page documents. It is often observed that employees do not read these lengthy documents as they are exceedingly difficult to refer to when needing to find specific information.

Map the process out or map each step out them out using tools such as flowcharts, swim lane diagrams, or process maps. This helps to visualize the sequence of tasks, roles, inputs, outputs, and dependencies involved in each process.

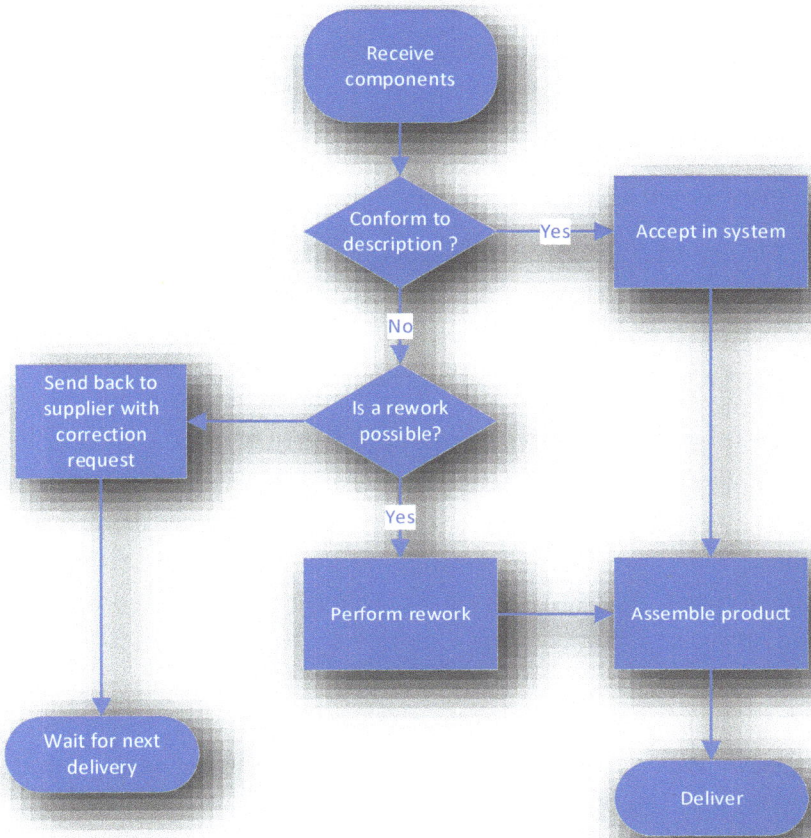

Process Map Example

In the one-page document summary, it is also important to stipulate the owner. This is an individual who is in a management role, who is accountable for making sure that people know about this document, are trained, and manage any changes needed to the process. We sometimes call this roe te process owner.

Introduce Short-Term Alignment Practices

Once people are aware of the process, we need to monitor them, make sure that they are adequate, and improve them when needed. Take note, we are saying **when** needed, and not **if** needed.

As Heraclitus wrote in 500 BC, *nothing is permanent except change*. An alignment of these processes or practices will always be needed as customers, needs, and technologies change.

So, how do we manage this alignment?

1. **Ensure that the process is documented.**
2. **Ensure that there is a process owner!**
3. **Establish one or two metrics with the process owner and start monitoring them on a regular basis.**

It might be tempting to add multiple metrics, some measuring the output (key performance indicators) and some measuring what is happening within the process (key process indicator). This will evolve with time, but starting to measure is already a big achievement. As a business starts to monitor how they are doing, measuring too many things could lead to bureaucracy and over processing. From personal experience, I worked in the quality department of an aerospace company where every quality engineer was spending more than 25 hours per week gathering metrics and building reports, therefore not leaving much time for corrective or preventive actions.

In terms of frequency of monitoring, it is recommended to start weekly, then increase or decrease the frequency depending on the observed performance. Please note that monitoring these processes monthly as part of some monthly management meeting is not a good idea since it would be too late and we would only see the result of the month. We would not know dynamically what is happening within a particular process, only the overall results. Hence, quality problems, delivery problems, or cost overruns would already have happened and impacted their business. As Edward Deming suggested, focusing only on results is like trying to drive a car while only looking in the rear view mirror.

4. **Identify and prioritize the gaps.**

As seen in the previous chapter, tools like the benefit versus effort matrix can be used. We can also dive deeper into prioritization using weighted matrices, as illustrated in the example below. We need to establish a set of criteria and relative importance with the management team as we need to create a consensus. We are also creating the basis of a regular management reviews where opportunities for improvement would be discussed. . In the example below, we used a score of 1 to 5 for the criteria, and in terms of scoring, we used the 0139 method to evaluate each identified project for each criterion.

- 0 - no impact
- 1 - low impact
- 3 - medium impact
- 9 - high impact

The total score for each project is the product of the score times the weight. We clearly see that the first project would be on the patient safety alert system.

	Patient's satisfaction	Infection prevention	Productivity	Capacity	Error prevention	Score
Weight	5	3	2	2	4	
3P for new wing layout	3	3	9	9	3	72
Patient safety alert system	3	9	3	1	9	86
Admittance process	3	0	3	3	1	31
Bed allocation process	3	1	3	9	3	54
Room cleaning process review	1	9	1	1	1	40

Weighted matrix example for a hospital

Another prioritization method is a value stream map that will be presented further below. As the first step, it is recommended to use a weighted matrix or the benefit versus effort matrix due to the relative simplicity of these tools.

A Note on Improvement Toolboxes and Methodologies

Although many improvement tools are presented in this book, exhaustive trainings and methodologies are available online and in classrooms. The most common ones are referred to as Lean, Six Sigma, and Lean Six Sigma. The advantage of these toolboxes is that their methodologies can be applied step by step for an extremely specific project. They all originate from the methodology that Edward Deming and Joseph Juran developed in Japan after the Second World War. The outcome of their methodology is what Toyota has termed Kaizen, translating to "change for the better," also known as continuous improvement. For a few decades, the rest of the world did not see an advantage in the adoption of these methods, until everyone was surprised and impressed by the quality and performance of Japanese products.

James Womack from Massachusetts Institute of Technology (MIT) introduced Kaizen and Lean to North America in the 1980's.

The steps of the **Lean Methodology** (1) are described below.

1. Define the problem and the goal

The team should identify the current state of the process or area, the issues or challenges that need to be addressed, and the desired future state or outcome. The problem and the goal should be clear, specific, and measurable.

2. Analyze the current situation and collect data

The team should observe and document the current process or area, using tools such as process maps, value stream maps, flowcharts, fishbone diagrams, or 5-Whys. The team should also collect and analyze data on key performance indicators, such as cycle time, defect rate, customer satisfaction, or productivity.

3. Generate and evaluate ideas for improvement

The team should brainstorm and list possible solutions or changes that can address the root causes of the problem and achieve the goal. The team should then evaluate the feasibility, impact, and cost-effectiveness of each idea, using tools such as benefit versus effort matrix, weighted matrix, or Pareto chart. In this step, there is a big focus on waste reduction (Muda).

4. Implement and evaluate the selected solution

The team should plan and execute the implementation of the chosen solution, using tools such as action plans, Gantt charts, or PDCA cycles. The team should also monitor and measure the results of the change, using tools such as control charts.

5. Standardize and sustain the improvement

The team should document and communicate the new process or area, using tools such as standard operating procedures, checklists, or visual aids. The team should also train and involve the relevant stakeholders, such as employees, customers, or suppliers, to ensure the adoption and maintenance of the improvement. The team should also celebrate and recognize the achievements and learnings from the improvement activity.

In the 1990s, Motorola, which was an early adopter of the Lean methodology, added another layer to the toolbox, and called it Six Sigma (2). This additional layer consisted of deeper root cause analysis, understanding variation, data analysis, and statistical analysis. Although the additions were extremely helpful, it caused some confusion in many companies. As an example, at Bombardier Aerospace, in the early 2000s, we could find both Lean improvement teams and Six Sigma improvement teams. This caused unnecessary discussions and delays in terms of which team would help with what type of projects.

Today, the most accepted name for the methodology is Lean Six Sigma (3) . The Lean Six Sigma methodology consists of six phases: Recognize, Define, Measure, Analyze, Improve, and Control (RDMAIC). As you will see below, these steps, apart from the first one, are remarkably close to what was already described for Lean.

1. Recognize

We start by identifying all the problems and opportunities and prioritizing them. Think about what was covered so far in this book!

2. Define

The team defines the scope and objectives of the project and establishes customer requirements and expectations.

3. Measure

In this phase, the team collects relevant information, data, and metrics to assess the current process and its performance. Here, we are looking for waste and variation.

4. Analyze

The team identifies the root causes of the waste or variation. The team also evaluates hypotheses and verifies the relationships between the process inputs and outputs.

5. Improve

Then the team generates and evaluates potential solutions to address the root causes and improve the process. The team also implements the selected solution and verifies the results and benefits.

6. Control

The team not only standardizes and documents the new process but also ensures effective communication and knowledge transfer, disseminating best practices across other processes or areas.

Lean Six Sigma methodology

The typical tools that are used within the methodology or shown per phase in the diagram above. Please note that all these tools were not created by Deming and Juran! There is for example the Pareto chart from Vilfredo Pareto, the Pugh matrix from Stewart Pugh, the SCAMPER analysis from Alex Osborne, the Ishikawa diagram from Kaoru Ishikawa, the five why from Sakichi Toyoda, etc.

Training and available certifications

As mentioned above, training is widely available. There are multiple levels of training and certification. Please note, there is no International Association who owns the overall certification. Some good sources for certifications are universities who have been providing the training for over 20, the Council for Six Sigma Certification, and the American Society for Quality.

A Lean Six Sigma White Belt is a person who has a basic understanding of the Lean Six Sigma principles and can support improvement projects as a team member or a sponsor.

A Lean Six Sigma Yellow Belt is a person who has more in-depth knowledge of the Lean Six Sigma methodology and can lead small-scale improvement projects within their own area of responsibility.

A Lean Six Sigma Green Belt is a person who has a comprehensive knowledge of the Lean Six Sigma methodology and can lead complex improvement projects across different functions or departments.

A Lean Six Sigma Black Belt is a person who has an expert level of knowledge of the Lean Six Sigma methodology and can lead strategic improvement initiatives that have a high impact on the organization's performance.

A Lean Six Sigma Master Black Belt is a person who has a mastery of the Lean Six Sigma methodology and can train, coach, and mentor other belts and facilitate the deployment of the Lean Six Sigma culture within the organization.

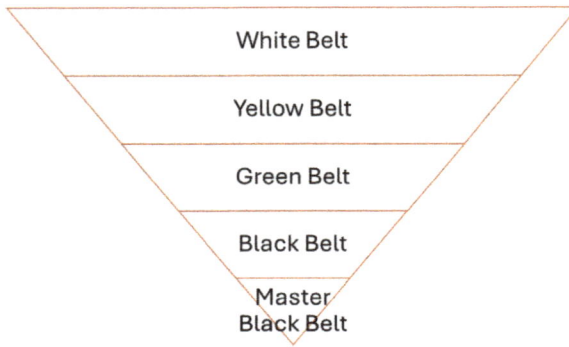

Hierarchy of Lean Six Sigma trainings and certifications

In this chapter, we detailed the practices needed to let the value stream in the organization and introduced some elements of the toolkit.

References

(1), The Toyota Way, Jeffrey Liker

(2) Six Sigma: The Breakthrough Management Strategy Revolutionizing the World's Top Corporations, Mikel Harry

(3) Practitioner's Guide to Statistics and Lean Six Sigma for Process Improvements, Mikel Harry

Achieving Excellence Roadmap

Define and Focus on the Value Provided to the Customer

- Review the teams, structure, team roles
- Elevate leadership
- Focus on Psychology and change management
- Identify quick wins, quick improvements
- Implement Agile practices: adaptability, communication, KPIs

Define and Understand How the Value Streams

- Understand and improve the processes
- Introduce Short term alignment practices
- Introduce value stream mapping

Innovate and Design

- Understand variation
- Compensate for variation
- Reduce variation: VOC, process mapping, analysis
- Learn from the hidden champions

Optimize the Flow

- Work to takt time
- Build models for the key processes

Become Demand Focused

- Plan for every request
- Introduce Pull
- Foster a culture of continuous progress

Total People Involvement   Voice of the Customer, Employees, Partners

76

Chapter 8 – Define and Understand How the Value Streams – Improvement Tools

In this chapter, we will detail key improvement tools available with many situational examples and recommendations. We will also cover value stream mapping and how to introduce it in the organization.

Key Improvement Tools

Whatever methodology is chosen, there are key tools that are always used due to their efficiency and effectiveness. We already introduced the benefit vs effort matrix, waste identification, and SCAMPER. Here are a few more that should not be missed.

Brainstorming and the affinity diagram

Brainstorming and the affinity diagram are two complementary tools that can help to generate and organize ideas for finding root causes of problems. Brainstorming is a technique that encourages participants to generate as many ideas as possible, without judging or evaluating them. The idea is to stimulate creativity and divergent thinking by allowing any suggestion, no matter how wild or unusual, to be expressed. Brainstorming can be done individually or in groups, using methods such as free association, mind mapping, or reverse brainstorming.

The affinity diagram is a tool that helps to sort and group the ideas generated by brainstorming into meaningful categories. The affinity diagram allows participants to see the relationships and patterns among the ideas, and to identify common themes or issues. The affinity diagram can also help to prioritize ideas and focus on the most relevant or important ones. The affinity diagram can be created by writing each idea on a sticky note or card and arranging them on a board or wall according to their affinity or similarity. The categories can be named and labeled accordingly.

We then vote and explore the top choices further. Following, we validate what we think is happening through observation, data collection, and then identifying low effort and high impact solutions.

By using brainstorming and the affinity diagram, one can find root causes of problems by generating many possible causes, and then grouping them into logical categories that reveal the underlying factors or sources of the problem. For example, if the problem is low customer satisfaction, one can brainstorm all the possible reasons why customers are dissatisfied, and then use the affinity diagram to sort them into categories such as product quality, service delivery, communication, pricing, etc. This can help to identify the main areas that need improvement and the root causes that affect them.

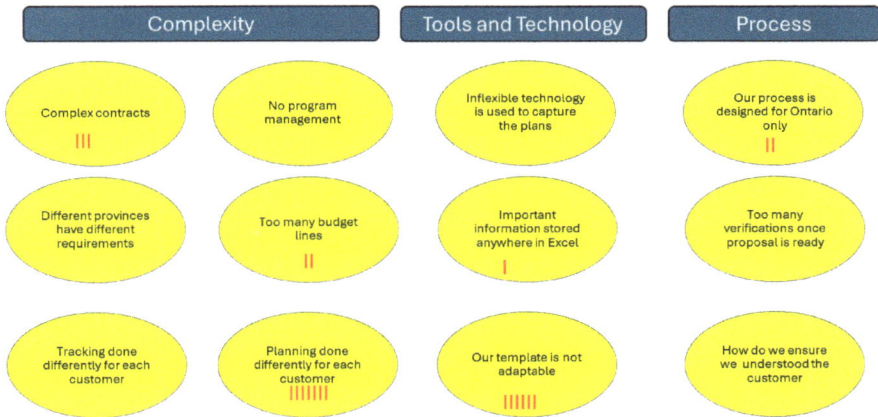

Complexity		Tools and Technology	Process
Complex contracts III	No program management	Inflexible technology is used to capture the plans	Our process is designed for Ontario only II
Different provinces have different requirements	Too many budget lines II	Important information stored anywhere in Excel I	Too many verifications once proposal is ready
Tracking done differently for each customer	Planning done differently for each customer IIIIIII	Our template is not adaptable IIIIII	How do we ensure we understood the customer

Affinity Diagram

78

Ishikawa diagram

The Ishikawa diagram, also known as the fishbone diagram or the cause-and-effect diagram, is a tool to identify the root causes of a problem by visualizing the relationship between the problem and its possible causes. The problem is represented as the head of the fish, and the main causes are represented as the bones. Each main cause can have sub-causes that branch out further. The Ishikawa diagram helps to organize the causes into categories, such as people, process, equipment, environment, etc., and to find the most significant factors that contribute to the problem.

The Ishikawa diagram is remarkably like the affinity diagram. One advantage that it has is to visually organize the relationship between the causes and the effect.

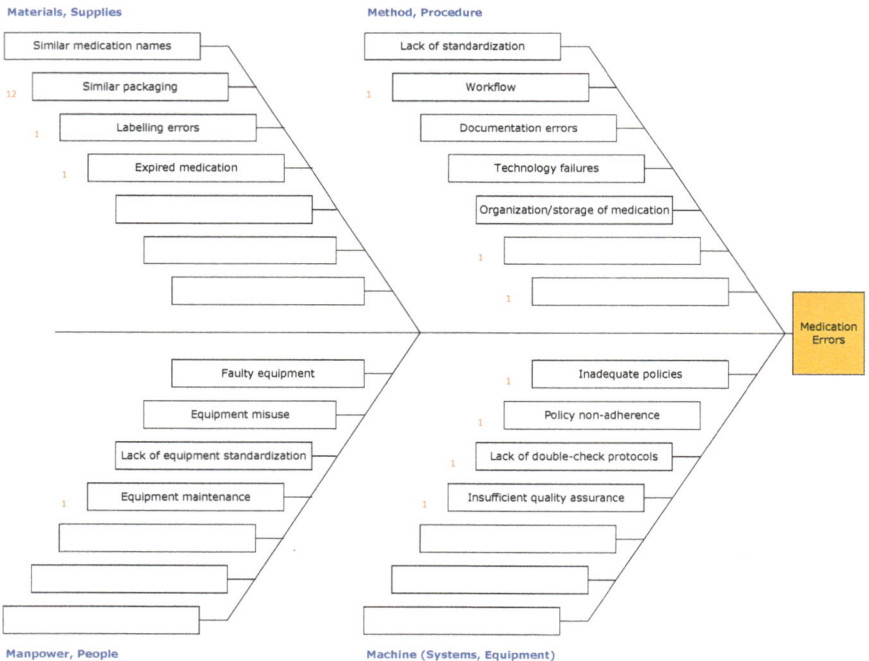

Materials, Supplies
- Similar medication names
- Similar packaging
- Labelling errors
- Expired medication

Method, Procedure
- Lack of standardization
- Workflow
- Documentation errors
- Technology failures
- Organization/storage of medication

Manpower, People
- Faulty equipment
- Equipment misuse
- Lack of equipment standardization
- Equipment maintenance

Machine (Systems, Equipment)
- Inadequate policies
- Policy non-adherence
- Lack of double-check protocols
- Insufficient quality assurance

Medication Errors

Ishikawa Diagram Example

79

Five why analysis

The five why analysis is a technique to find the root cause of a problem by asking "why" five times, or as many times as needed, until the underlying cause is revealed. It is often used after an Ishikawa diagram or an affinity diagram, which helps to identify the possible causes of a problem in different categories]. The five why analysis helps uncover the most significant or frequent causes and eliminate them. It is important to note that it can also extend to six or seven whys/ Additionally, stressing the significance of data collection and observation between each why is essential.

As an example, we worked on an issue with the quality of a patient support program call center.

Why is the call quality inconsistent?

→ *Because the possible answers are not standardized or documented.*

Why aren't the answers standardized or documented?

→ *Because it is believed that the answers would be easy for the healthcare professionals.*

Why is it is believed that the answers would be easy for the healthcare professionals?

→ *Because there were no surveys conducted regarding typical patient inquiries.*

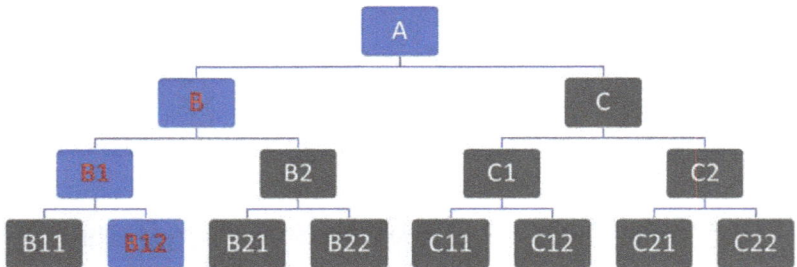

5 Whys elimination process

At each question, there might be multiple causes, and this is why it is important to get data before going to the next step. The five why is an elimination process. Although examining B or C and all their underlying causes to find the root cause of A would be a remarkably interesting exercise, it would be very tedious. Therefore, we can first validate if C is a cause. In this example, it is not, therefore we cross out that entire branch from our analysis.

Process Mapping

The process map is not only a tool to document the current state of a process, but also a powerful way to identify improvement opportunities and root causes of problems. By mapping out the steps, inputs, outputs, roles, and resources involved in a process, you can identify gaps, bottlenecks, redundancies, or delays that impact the quality, speed, or cost of the process. A process map can also help to analyze the impact of any changes or solutions that are proposed for the process.

In the map below, we can clearly observe that there is a lot of Muda that can be worked on.

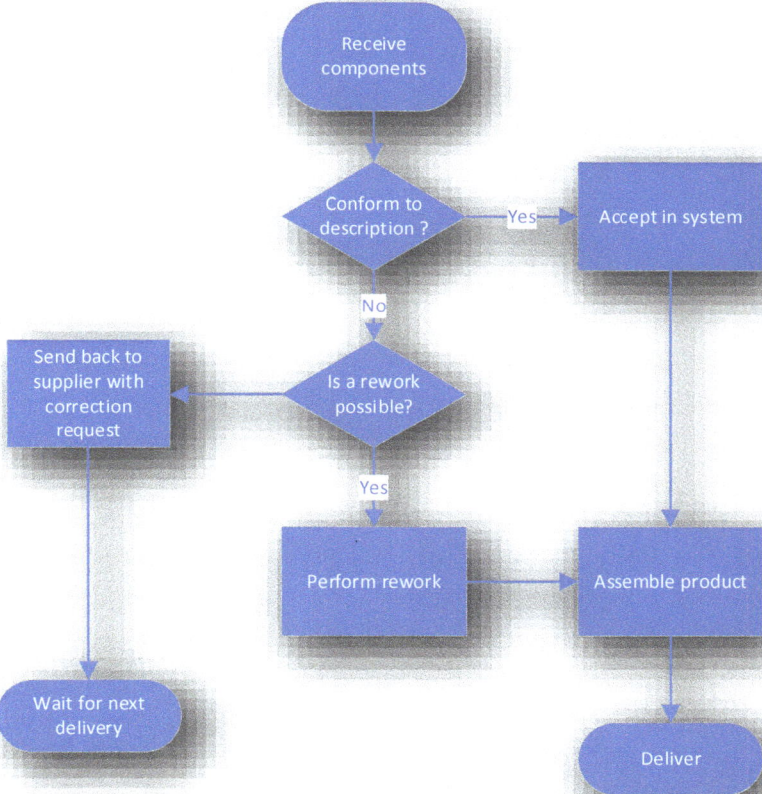

Process Map Example – Receiving Components

Let us break down some of these observations:

- Even though the process is clear, we might explore why we need to verify if the components are conformed to the description, how come we receive defects.
- Do we need to accept the material in the system or can this be done automatically?
- Why do we rework the defective components? This is a waste of money, time and energy, especially if we cannot charge back the rework time.
- We see delays can be caused by waiting for the next delivery.

Once the issues are identified, we can then validate them through observation, data collection, and then identifying low effort and high impact solutions.

Another example can be found below related to planned procedures. We can clearly observe that there is a lot of motion and waiting. Also, we do not plan early enough – planning the staff, the rooms, and if we need anesthesia or not. In this example, the staff received their schedule on Fridays, but were not notified of changes during the week, which leads to nurses and doctors showing up at the wrong times, or not showing up when needed.

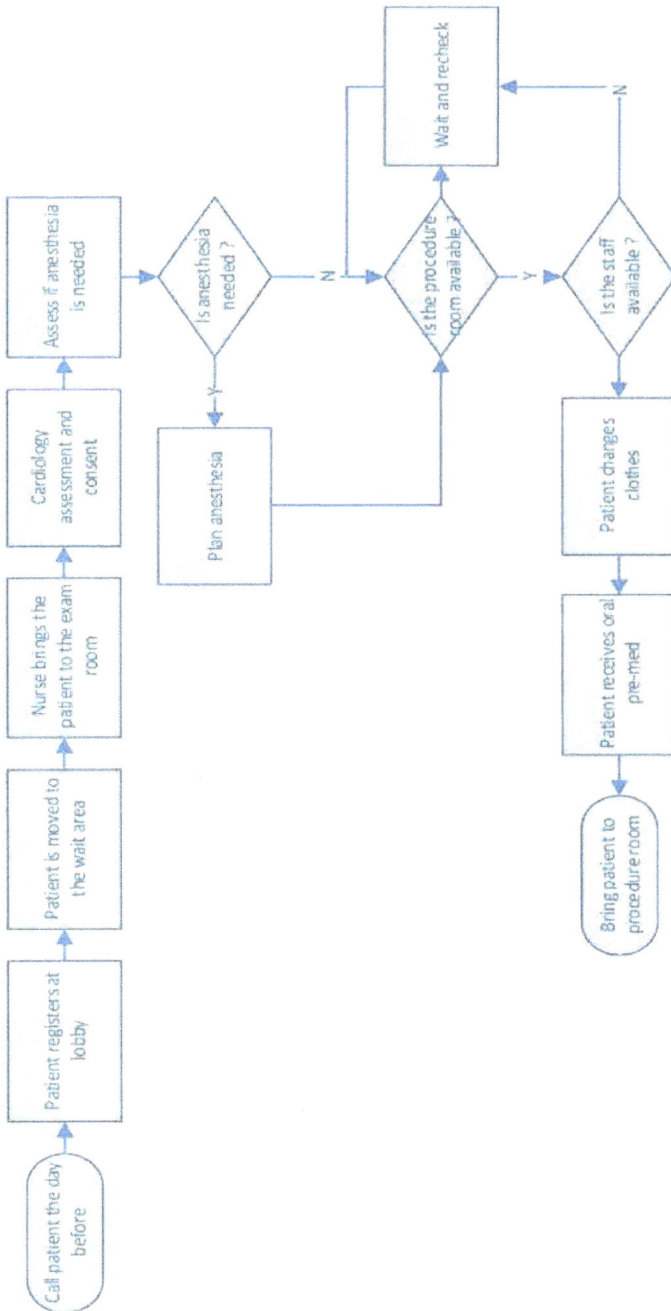

Process Map Example – Processing a Patient for a Procedure

Value Stream Mapping

Value stream mapping (1)(2) is a high level of representation of the value chain, composed of the core processes with some key metrics search as cycle times and delays. You might wonder why we are presenting this technique at the end of the chapter rather than at the beginning. Although it is a wonderful tool to prioritize process improvements and improvement projects, it requires that we first establish and standardize these processes to ensure we are consistently creating value.

A value stream map is a visual tool that shows the flow of value from the customer's perspective, as well as the waste and inefficiencies that occur along the way. A value stream map helps to identify the sources of variation, delay, and non-value added activities in a process, and to prioritize improvement opportunities.

The steps to create a value stream map are:

- Define the scope and purpose of the mapping exercise. Specify the product or service family, the customer segment, the start and end points, and the objective of the mapping.

- Identify the key stakeholders and form a cross-functional team. Involve people who have direct knowledge and experience of the process, as well as those who can provide support and resources.

- Collect data on the current state of the process. Use tools such as observations, interviews, surveys, documents, and metrics to gather information on the activities, resources, time, quality, costs, or other metrics such as customer satisfaction.

It is important as well to define Takt Time. Takt time is calculated by dividing the available working time by the number of units required by the customer in that time. For example, if a customer orders 100 units per day, and a factory operates for 8 hours per day, then the takt time is 8 hours / 100 units = 4.8 minutes per unit.

This means that the factory should produce one unit every 4.8 minutes to meet the customer demand. Takt time is the beat rate at which we need to deliver a product or service to a customer. Otherwise, we would be creating a backlog.

- Draw the current state map. Use standard symbols and conventions to represent the process steps, the flow of materials and information, the inventory and waiting times, and the performance indicators.

- Analyze the current state map and identify the bottleneck, problems, and issues.

- Envision and draw the future state of the process. Indicate the expected benefits and impacts of the future state on the performance indicators.

- Develop a value stream improvement plan, or implementation plan. List the projects, actions, responsibilities, and timeline needed to transform the current state into the future state.

In the following example of a restaurant, we see all the steps with some secret codes! Allow us to share the secret codes with you:

-   CT = Cycle Time – how long does the step take
-   SU = Setup Time – how long does it take us to set up in the morning or between shifts
-   Yield = Success Rate (100% - Defective %)
-   Batch = Number of requests, orders, or units that we can process concurrently
-   Δ = Inventory (WIP, or Work in Progress)

The timeline below consists of the cycle time and waiting times. The waiting time is calculated by multiplying the cycle time by the number of items in WIP and dividing by the batch. As an example, for the preparation step, the cycle time is 24 minutes, and there are four orders waiting. The waiting time is 24 X 4 which gives us

96 minutes. However, there are two chefs, so we divide the waiting time per two, which gives us 48 minutes.

The lead time is the typical total time for a typical customer which is 177 minutes. The process time is the time spent doing something, which is 54 minutes. The rest is waiting. The efficiency is the process time divided by the lead time, meaning we are doing something 46% of the time, or 54% of the time is just waiting time.

As the takt time is 10 minutes, we can conclude that we have many problems. As such, we will start with the bottleneck, preparation, which is the longest step. This is a key takeaway from building a value stream map, as it does point out to which processes to improve first and which ones will have the most benefit.

Looking at the preparation step, a simple solution would be to add staff. However, it would be more cost effective to first look at Muda to change how we prepare. We could also prepare certain items before the restaurant opens. Reducing the cycle time would result in reducing the waiting time as well. That is why we need to start with the bottleneck.

	Take order	Prep	Oven	Final prep	Deliver food
CT	5	24	17	6	2
SU	0	0	0	0	0
Yield	95%	90%	80%	85%	99%
Batch	2	2	5	1	2

Inventory: 2, 4, 1, 1, 1

Timeline: 5.0, 48, 24, 3.4, 17, 6, 6, 1, 2

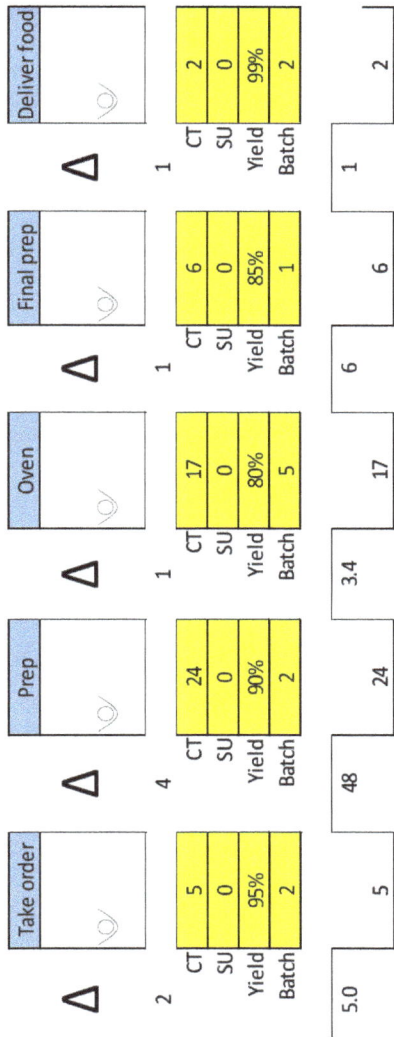

Process time	54
Lead time	117.4
Efficiency	46.0%

Takt time	10

Value Stream Map Example

88

We would then look at other problematic processes, one by one and drive improvements. The purpose of the value stream mapping exercise is to prioritize the improvement activities and opportunities, allowing us to address issues step by step rather than attempting to tackle everything at once. For each one of the improvements identified, we would typically need to go through workshops for improvement projects using the tools that we mentioned in this chapter.

Building a value stream map with a team can first look messy, and it is totally fine. The example below refers to assembling an aircraft once we get a customer order. This example was done as part of one of my classes as an operational strategy planning exercise at McGill University with experts from different aerospace organizations. As the team throws down their ideas and though, it builds a common understanding what are is the situation, what are the gaps, and what we wish to achieve. It becomes then very clear. We could of course making it much cleaner using value stream mapping software. The one on top was created with the Lean Six Sigma Companion.

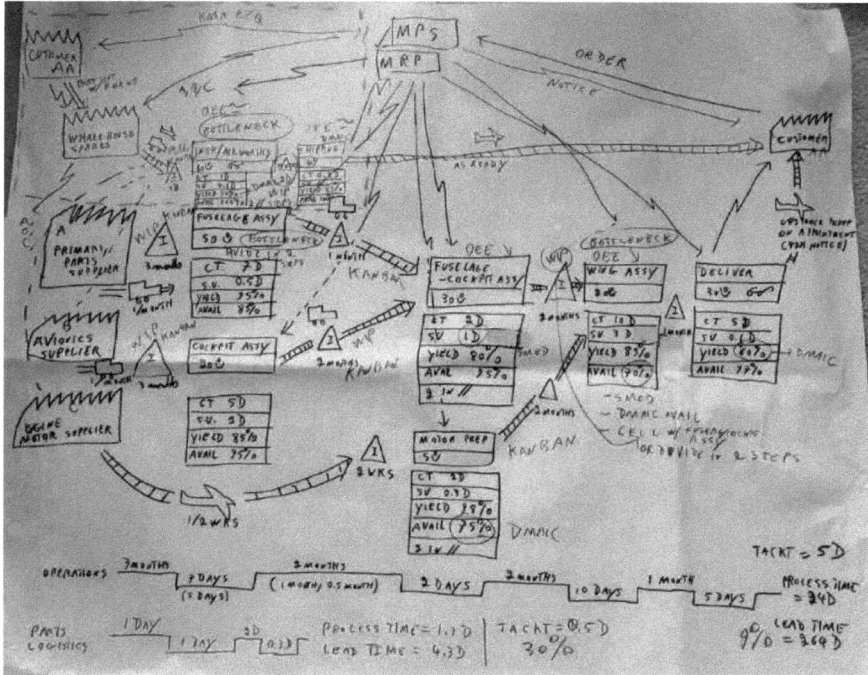

Value Stream Map Exercise – Aircraft Assembly

In this chapter, we introduced the concept of ensuring that the value streams. We also discussed short-term alignment practices through process ownership and monitoring. One step at a time!

References

(1) Learning to see Mike Rother
(2) Seeing the Whole: Mapping the Extended Value Stream, Daniel Jones

Achieving Excellence Roadmap

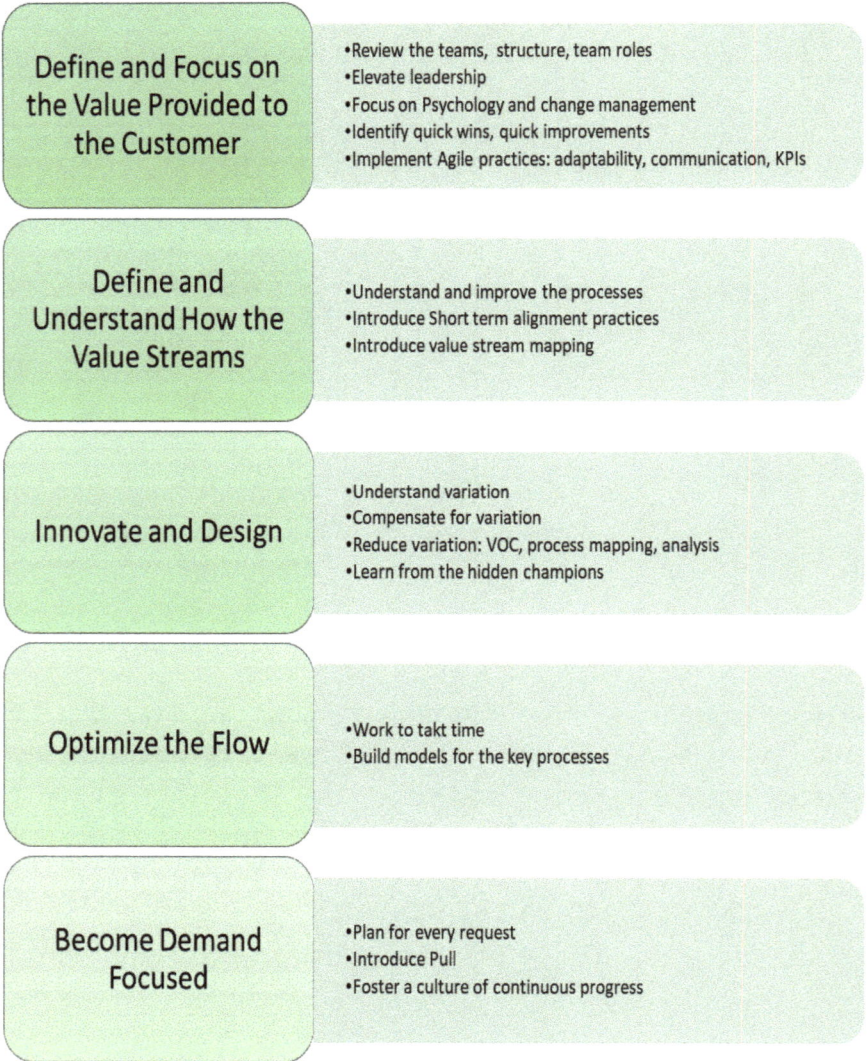

Define and Focus on the Value Provided to the Customer	• Review the teams, structure, team roles • Elevate leadership • Focus on Psychology and change management • Identify quick wins, quick improvements • Implement Agile practices: adaptability, communication, KPIs
Define and Understand How the Value Streams	• Understand and improve the processes • Introduce Short term alignment practices • Introduce value stream mapping
Innovate and Design	• Understand variation • Compensate for variation • Reduce variation: VOC, process mapping, analysis • Learn from the hidden champions
Optimize the Flow	• Work to takt time • Build models for the key processes
Become Demand Focused	• Plan for every request • Introduce Pull • Foster a culture of continuous progress

Total People Involvement   Voice of the Customer, Employees, Partners

Chapter 9 – Innovate and Design

Innovate and Design

- Understand variation
- Compensate for variation
- Reduce variation: VOC, process mapping, analysis
- Learn from the hidden champions

Now, we are at a point where our way of working is defined, and we have key processes that are performing well or to an acceptable level. What comes next? Of course, we need to continue to prioritize upcoming challenges, changes, and requests from the customers. With our experience in process definition and improvement, we can focus on understanding and managing consistency by examining variation. We'll explore the sources of variation and determine appropriate strategies for dealing with it – whether by coping with it, compensating for it, reducing it, or eliminating it entirely where possible.

We will also look at drastic process change, or innovation or "kaikaku" as the Japanese call it. *Innovation can involve technology and other aspects related to hidden champions – companies that are great at what they are doing but are unknown.*

Looking at our roadmap and what is in Innovate and Design, we will cover the first two topics in this chapter:

- Understanding variation
- Compensating for variation

Understanding Variation

As Einstein once said, *"If I had an hour to solve a problem and my life depended on the solution, I would spend the first 55 minutes determining the proper question to ask… for once I know the proper question, I could solve the problem in less than five minutes."*

Understanding is the first step. It is quite tempting to act right away. In this first section, we will introduce some key approaches to facilitate understanding and utilizing effectively.

To start, let's explore the concept of variation. Variation is the difference or deviation from a standard or expected value or condition. In Japanese, and it is always fun to know a bit of Japanese, it is defined as Mura.

In performance, variation can indicate how consistent or reliable a service or product is or how fast or slow a delivery time is. Understanding variation helps us identify the sources of variability, which can be either common causes inherent to the system or process, such as a slow internet connection, or special causes resulting from external factors or errors, like a power outage.

By understanding and reducing variation, we can improve the quality and efficiency of our performance and satisfy our customers' needs and expectations.

Five Whys Analysis and Data Collection

In the previous chapter, we already discussed the Five Whys analysis, which is a technique to find the root cause of a problem by asking "why" five times, or as many times as needed, until the underlying cause is revealed. The Five Whys technique requires the incorporation of data, facts, and information between each of the questions to avoid making assumptions about the causes. First, we need to find out if the data is readily available in a system or database. Secondly, we need to make sure that this data is useful and provides us with the insights we need.

The example below illustrates deliveries of control system components, which are used to monitor and control the flow of chemical processes. In the ERP system (Enterprise Resource Planning), we had information related to the three columns on the left, which pertain to the orders that were placed. To compare the planned budget with the actual spending, we needed to ask the project managers and various stakeholders in the organization for specific data related to the budget and its variance. Please note that in this data collection, we used the word "delta" instead of variance as the team members might have been confused between variance and variation. As we were getting that information from the project managers, we also asked them for a high-level reason that would explain the difference in their budget. Although these comments are somewhat general and subjective, we can ask more detailed questions to drill down deeper into the underlying causes. The example shown below is a short extract of the full data collection. Sometimes, the data or information can be missing in the 'reason given' column. If a project cannot remember the reason, it would require further investigation to complete this data collection.

Customer	Type	Date	Budget	Delta vs Budget	Reason given
SNC	Regulators	January	60K	20K	Wrong specification
Kraft	Valves	January	8K	Positive 2K	Productive team
SNC	Mixed	February	200K	60K	Wrong specification
Hatch	Regulators	March	25K	4K	Poor evaluation
Veolia	Controllers	June	210K	Positive 4K	Productive team
Kraft	Valves	June	8K	0K	
Hatch	Regulators	September	25K	6K	Optimistic assessment
SNC	Controllers	December	180K	65K	Wrong specification

Data collection – budget and variance to the budget

Data collection can be challenging and time-consuming. As such, we often rely on sampling instead of gathering exhaustive data.

We also need to ensure that we have the correct data collection tools and the correct reports or measurements. In case of doubt, it is recommended to use different methods to validate if the data is consistent or not. To highlight the importance of validation, try counting how many times the letter 'F' appears in the text below.

The First Necessity of Training Farm Hands for First Class Farms in the Fatherly Handling of Farm livestock is foremost in the Eyes of Farm Owners. Since the Forefathers of the Farm Owners Trained the Farm Hands for First Class Farms in the Fatherly Handling of Farm Live Stock, the Fellow Farm Owners Feel they should carry on with the Family Tradition of Training Farm Hands of First Class Farmers in the Fatherly Handling of Farm Live Stock because they believe it is the Basis of Good Fundamentals of Farm Management.

Different people get different answers. This text is designed to be difficult to read, and many people miss the lowercase letters, especially when they are in front of uppercase letters. You might argue that this can easily be counted using Microsoft Word's 'find' function. Curiously, different versions of Microsoft Office provide different answers overtime. In the current version that I am using, the answer is 39, although when I ran the same function in 2008, the answer was 38! At the time that we are writing this book, ChatGPT is giving us an answer of 22. How many 'F's did you find?

Pareto Charts, Pie Charts & Line Graphs

Once the data is available, it could be an eyesore to look at all the columns of numbers and facts. Think about using graphs to easily grasp what the data is saying, as well as communicate what we discovered to the stakeholders and team members. We can utilize pie charts, line graphs, Pareto charts, and so many others.

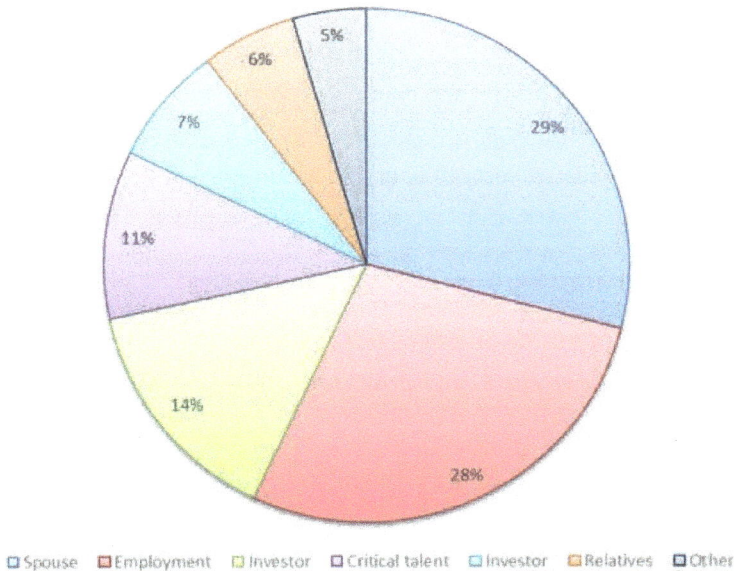

□ Spouse □ Employment □ Investor □ Critical talent □ Investor □ Relatives □ Other

Pie chart example

Let's first review the pie chart.

A pie chart is a type of graph that shows the relative proportions of different categories or parts of a whole. The chart is divided into sectors, or slices, that represent each category's percentage of the total. A pie chart is useful for comparing the sizes of different groups and highlighting the largest or smallest ones. However, a pie chart can also have some limitations, such as showing too many categories or obscuring small differences. In the example above, statistics related to immigration, we can see that spousal immigration counts for 29%, followed by employment and the other categories.

A variation to the pie chart is the Pareto chart, which is a type of bar graph that shows the frequency or count of different categories or causes of a problem, along with a line that shows the cumulative percentage of the total. The chart is based on the principle that a few categories or causes are responsible for most of the problems or effects. By focusing on them, we can achieve the greatest improvement. This principle is also known as the 80/20 rule, or the Pareto principle, named after the Italian economist Vilfredo Pareto.

A Pareto chart has some advantages over a pie chart, such as:

- It can show more than one variable, such as the frequency and the percentage, while a pie chart can only show one variable as slices of a circle.

- It can rank the categories or causes in descending order, which makes it easier to identify and prioritize the most important ones, while a pie chart does not have a natural order and may require labels or legends to explain the slices.

- It can handle large numbers of categories or causes, while a pie chart becomes cluttered and unreadable when there are too many slices.

In the example below, we can easily see that the address and price are the largest causes, and the cumulative percentage shows us that these two account for roughly 90% of the defects.

We typically use pie charts or Pareto charts without looking at trends over time. This is a big miss!

This brings us to the next graph. One of the advantages of using a line graph to see trends over time is that it can help to identify patterns and anomalies in the data. A line graph can show how a variable changes over time, whether it is increasing, decreasing, or fluctuating. It can also show the relationship between two or more variables, such as sales and defects, and how they affect each other. A line graph can reveal seasonal variations, cyclical trends, peaks and troughs, and outliers. By looking at a line graph, we can ask questions about the causes and effects of the changes in the data and use this information to make decisions and improvements.

A Pareto chart or a pie chart, on the other hand, can only show the relative frequency or proportion of different categories of data at a given point in time. They cannot show how the data changes over time or how different categories are related to each other. They can only show which categories are significant, but not why or how. A Pareto chart or a pie chart can be useful for prioritizing problems or opportunities, but they do not provide enough information to understand the underlying trends and dynamics of the data.

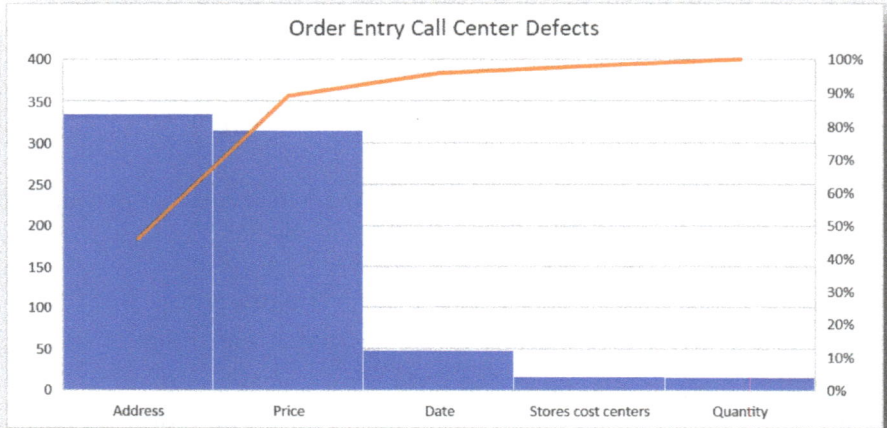

Pareto chart example

Let us continue with the order entry call centre defects example depicted above. We have already learned from the Pareto chart that the largest contributors to the defects are the address and price. Looking at the line graphs below, we see the behaviour over 10 weeks. The volume of calls is similar from week to week. Otherwise, we would need to take a proportion of the defects on the number of calls.

We can see that the price defects tend to be quite stable, between 20 and 40 defects per week. However, there is a lot of variation in terms of the address defects, going from 5 to 70. We can also observe a cycle as the defects are very high in week 1, then go down, go back up to a maximum, and then go back down. We may not have enough data to be completely certain that a cycle exists, but we do have sufficient findings to ask people about events during specific weeks. By doing so, we can learn from their responses.

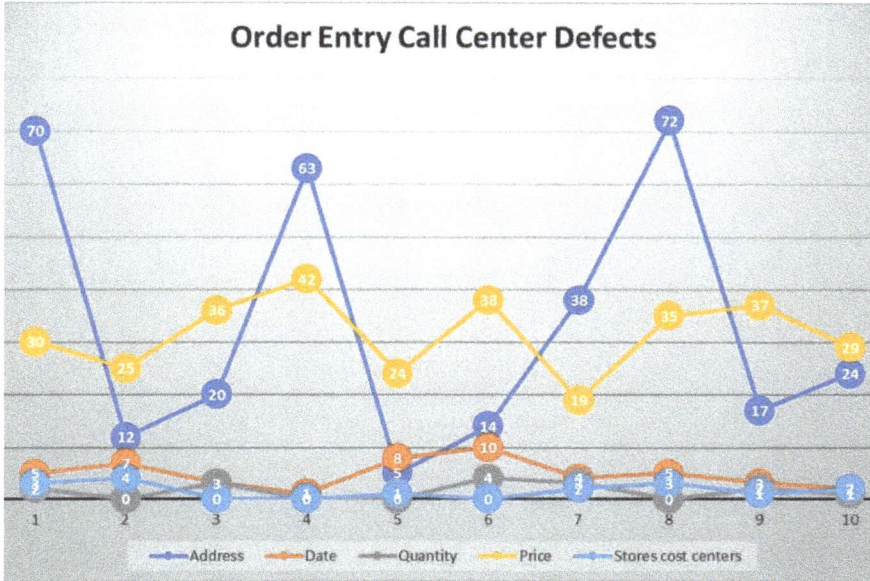

Order Entry Call Center Defects

Line Graph – Order entry defects

Graphing the Data – Learning More About Variation

Some more complex graphs can give us a deeper understanding of our variation. We might wish to know how much variation is at play and how it affects us. We cannot rely solely on averages to make decisions. Let's take a simple example. It is December 10th, and we would like to order Christmas gifts. We need to ensure that we have them before December 24th. If Supplier 1 has an average delivery time of 12 days and Supplier 2 has an average delivery time of 10 days, which one would you pick? On the surface, it seems obvious to go with Supplier 2. Now, let's add the variation component. In the picture below, we see the distributions representing the historical performance of these two suppliers. We see that although Supplier 2 is quicker, there is much more variation. We can express the variation by calculating the standard deviation – the larger it is, the more variation is at play. Now, with this full information, which one would you choose to reduce the risk and ensure that we receive all the gifts by our deadline of December 24th? Supplier 1 would be the best choice.

Average vs Variation

Using statistical analysis, we can even estimate what percentage of

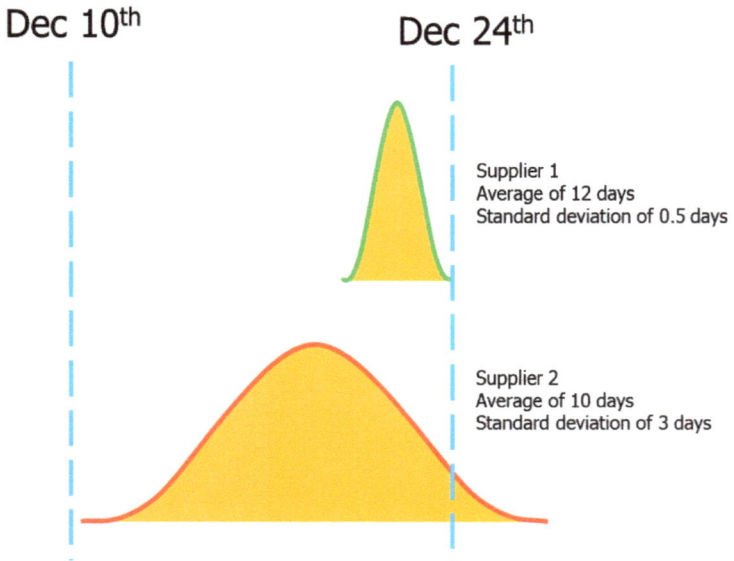

Dec 10th   Dec 24th

Supplier 1
Average of 12 days
Standard deviation of 0.5 days

Supplier 2
Average of 10 days
Standard deviation of 3 days

orders would meet the deadline. This is what we call process performance or process capability. The example below is based on the Lean Six Sigma Companion Templates (9.1), available on our website. The tool calculates the probability of meeting the Upper Specification Limit, which is our maximum of 14 days (December 24th minus December 10th), given the historical performance. We see that the success rate (yield) is 90.4%. In other words, 9.6% of the deliveries will be late, which is note great. The yield corresponds to a sigma level, which is another way to look at the performance. We can see that the sigma level here is 1.31. A sigma level of 6 (six sigma) is 99.9996%.

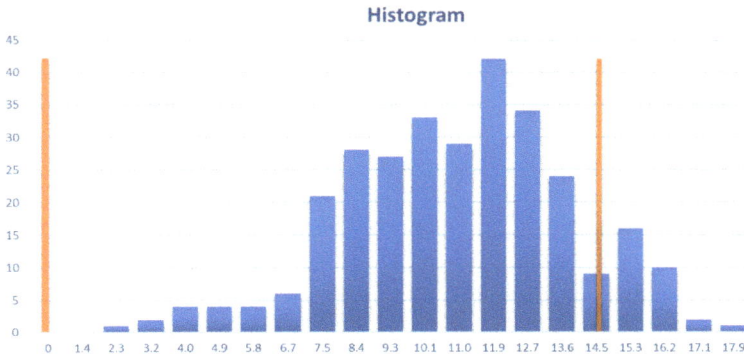

Histogram

Statistics and Process Capability Report						
average	10.14	Cp	0.79	Z short term	1.31	or Sigma level
std dev	2.95	Cpk lower	1.15	Yield short term	90.490%	
LSL	0.00	Cpk upper	0.44	Z long term	-0.1900	or Sigma level
USL	14.00	Cpk	0.44	Yield long term	42.466%	
		Ppk with 0.5 shift	-0.06			

Example of process capability

We can also compare the performance of different processes or suppliers using the boxplot in Microsoft Excel or with the Lean Six Sigma Companion template (9.1).

A boxplot starts with a box that represents 50% of the data around the median. The line, or whiskers, is the rest of the data. The example below shows how much time patients have been waiting in an emergency department. Between 2018 and 2019, the admission and triage processes were changed. We see that the time is slightly shorter in 2019, but we have more variation. Thus, we can conclude that the new process is better; however can still use some improvement.

This type of comparison should be done between the actual and improved processes. We can also compare Pareto charts and line graphs.

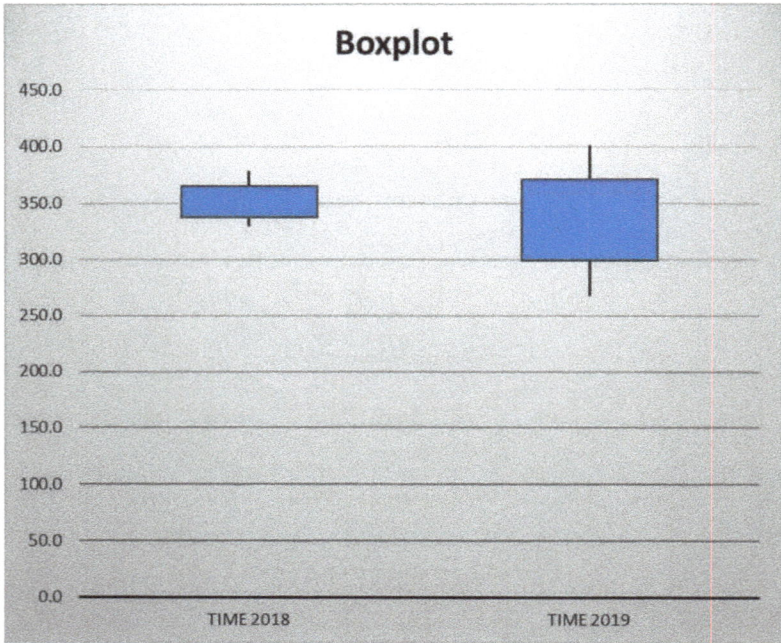

Boxplot

Boxplot comparing the 2018 method to the 2019 method.

Statistical Tests

Now, what if the process measured in 2019 cost hundreds of thousands of dollars to deploy to other locations in this hospital network? Would it be worth it? How can we be sure? Graphs are great sometimes but insufficient when there is a high cost, high effort, or high level of risk. As such, we can complement this type of analysis with statistical tests.

One of the most common statistical tests is the t-test.

A t-test is a statistical method that compares the means of two groups of data and determines if they are significantly different from each other. A t-test can help us answer questions such as: is the average length of stay of patients in 2019 lower than in 2018? A t-test can also tell us how confident we are about the difference by providing a p-value that indicates the probability of observing such a difference by chance. The lower the p-value, the more confident we are that the difference is real and not due to random variation. We typically look for p-values lower than 0.05 (5%).

Let's break down the following example that was built with the Lean Six Sigma Companion (9.1). Look at the first line of the t-test, "unequal variance", which is the one that we generally pick. Variance is the square of the standard deviation, and we choose "unequal variance" if we have not compared the variances between the two data sets. Alternatively, we would choose "equal variance" if we know that the variances are equal. This part will be covered in the next chapter with the f-Test. "Paired" would mean that data from 2018 and 2019 is paired. As an example, we can compare the waiting time of patient Steven in 2018 vs. 2019 and then the waiting time of patient Sara in 2019 vs. 2019. The p-value is 0.028. Therefore we can be confident that the average is better (lower) in 2019. We see the averages as well as the confidence interval (CI). The t-test tells us that based on the data available, the average is definitely between 314 minutes and 347 minutes.

t - test

1 or 2 tails	2

Take 2 tails by default and unequal variance

Confidence Intervals and statistics

	Time 2018	Time 2019
Alpha	0.05	0.05
n samples	29	29

t-test	Unequal variance	0.028
t-test	Equal Variance	0.026
t-test	Paired	0.017

There is a significant difference if result is lower than 0.05

	Time 2018	Time 2019
Average	351.80	331.09
Std dev	21.40	44.01
CI	8.1	16.7
Lower CI	343.7	314.3
Upper CI	359.9	347.8

T-test on the waiting time

Compensating for Variation

Muda, also known as non-value-added activities, are typically much easier to reduce or eliminate than variation. For example, if there is too much paperwork transportation, we can digitize the process, reduce the number of signatures, create digital signatures, etc. On the other hand, in a production environment, variation needs a deep dive in terms of the contributing causes. This may mean utilizing statistical analysis tools, changes in process, or technology.

Remember that Muda (waste) and Mura (variation) are related. Thus, we should always start by reducing Muda. For example, if we consider the variation in waiting times for patients in a clinic or customers in a bank, we start by ensuring that the staff have everything they need at their workstations – information, paperwork, tools, gloves, etc. By doing so, motion and transport are minimized, which reduces waiting times and, consequently, further decreases overall waiting.

Once we reduce waste, we then tackle variation with 4 tactics:

1. Sorting, selection, inspection
2. Control charts and tracking
3. Poka Yoke
4. Statistical analysis

We will discuss the first three in this chapter.

Sorting, Selection, Inspection

One of the common methods to ensure the quality of the products or services is inspection. Inspection involves checking the output for defects or errors and removing the faulty ones from the process. For example; a car manufacturer may inspect the cars for any defects before they are shipped to the dealers. Inspection can help reduce customer complaints, improve customer satisfaction, and comply with the standards and regulations. Inspection applies to any type of transaction, service, document generation, software, etc.

Despite its benefits, relying solely on inspections to ensure quality can be problematic. Inspection has many drawbacks, especially in terms of added costs and inefficiencies. Inspection does not improve the process itself but only manages the output. It does not address the root causes of the problems, as it deals only with the defects. Inspection also requires extra resources, such as time, labor, equipment, and space, which can increase operational costs and reduce productivity.

Therefore, inspection should not be the sole method of quality control but rather a complementary one that is combined with other techniques, such as prevention and improvement.

Inspection does involve sorting what is good and what is defective, and reworking document mistakes and defective parts. In many cases, physical parts would be scrapped as they cannot be reworked. Lots of extra costs!

An interesting case can be observed in manufacturing assembly processes, specifically in part selection. We might have many defective parts – some too small or too big – but we can match them to ensure correctness. Let's walk through a simple example, referencing the picture below. Ideally, parts A and B have the right dimensions, including their lengths. However, due to process variation, we might end up with parts that are right, too small, or too large.

We can sort the parts, keep the ones that are the best, and dispose of the ones that are way too small or way too big. We can always try to add some shims or press hard to make the parts fit. However, all of these solutions add extra work. One technique is to mix and match the parts. We would match the small A with the small B and the large A with the large B. This is a simplification. In a real situation, we would have 5 or 10 categories, such as going from extra-small to extra-large. This technique helps to reuse the parts and to reduce scrap. It helps to compensate for variation, although it introduces another Muda, overprocessing. Nonetheless, it is a lesser evil.

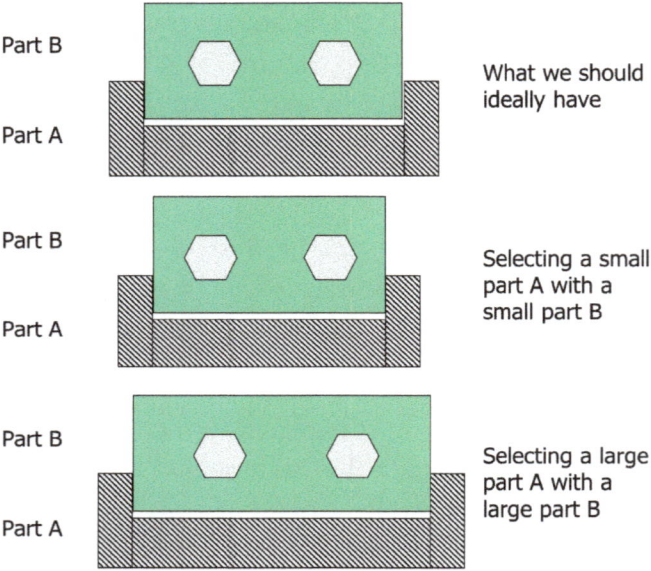

Part selection –simple example

Control Charts and Tracking

We can monitor the variation over time in a simple and effective way using control charts. This would enable us to see trends and take appropriate actions.

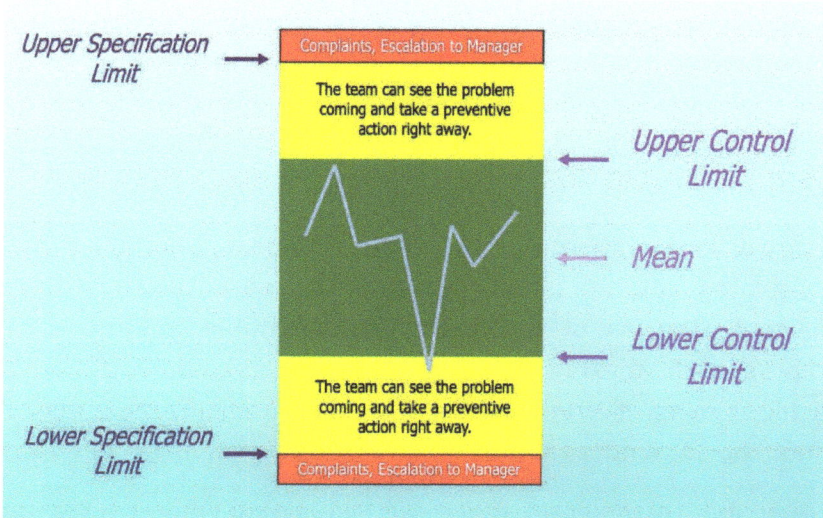

Upper Specification Limit → Complaints, Escalation to Manager

The team can see the problem coming and take a preventive action right away.

← **Upper Control Limit**

←— **Mean**

← **Lower Control Limit**

The team can see the problem coming and take a preventive action right away.

Lower Specification Limit → Complaints, Escalation to Manager

Specification limits and control limits

A control chart is a graphical tool that displays the variation of a process over time and compares it to predefined limits. These limits, also called control limits, are calculated based on the historical data of the process and represent the expected range of variation under normal conditions.

Specification limits and control limits are two different concepts that are often confused. Specification limits are the requirements or targets that are set by the customer or the organization for the quality of a product or service. They represent the desired level of performance or the acceptable range of variation for a certain characteristic. For example, if a customer wants an order delivered within 30 minutes, then the specification limit for the delivery time is 30 minutes. Specification limits are not based on historical data of the process but on the expectations or needs of the customer or the organization. In this example, there is only an upper specification limit set at a maximum acceptable of 30 minutes. We can also have a lower specification limit. For instance, when considering the battery life of a laptop, one might expect a minimum of 10 hours before needing to recharge it. Sometimes, we may also have both an upper specification limit and a lower specification limit. For example, indoor temperature falls between 19°C and 21°C.

Control limits, on the other hand, are the boundaries that are calculated from the historical data of the process and indicate the natural variation of the process under stable conditions. They represent the maximum and minimum values that the process can achieve when it is in control. Using the order example above, it could be 15 minutes and 25 minutes.

Looking at the diagram above, we take action when we are in the yellow zone before reaching the red. Control charts and control limits allow us to act preventively.

There are multiple types of control charts. One of the most common types of control charts is the X-bar and R-control chart, used to monitor the variation of processes that produce continuous data – anything measurable on a scale from small to large, such as waiting time, response time, length, weight, temperature, or monetary values. The X-bar and R control chart consists of two sub-charts: one for the average (X-bar) and one for the Range (r) of each subgroup of data. The range is the difference between the maximum and minimum values in each subgroup. In other terms, we are monitoring the average performance of a process and its variation.

The control limits for the X-bar and R-control charts are typically calculated using the following formulas.

- Upper control limit for X bar = average + 3 X standard deviation
  Lower control limit for X bar = average - 3 X standard deviation
- Upper control limit for R = 2 * the average of ranges
  (this is a simplification)
- Lower control limit for R = 0
  (this is a simplification)

The formula for the standard deviation is included below as a reference. We typically use tools to calculate it, as it can be quite long to do it by hand. It is a measure of variation or deviation from a standard or expected value or condition. The larger the standard deviation, the more variation we have.

$$S = \sigma_{est} = \sqrt{\frac{1}{n-1}\sum_{i=1}^{n}(x_i - \bar{x})^2}$$

Please note that it is recommended to use tools such as the Lean Six Sigma Companion templates (9.1) or Minitab to get the exact control limit calculations.

The control limits are drawn as horizontal lines on the chart, along with the centre line, which is the average (X-bar) or average of ranges (R-bar). The subgroups are plotted in chronological order and connected by a line. If any points fall outside the control limits or show a non-random pattern, such as a run of seven consecutive points above or below the centre line, it indicates that the process is out of control and there is a special cause of variation that needs to be investigated and eliminated.

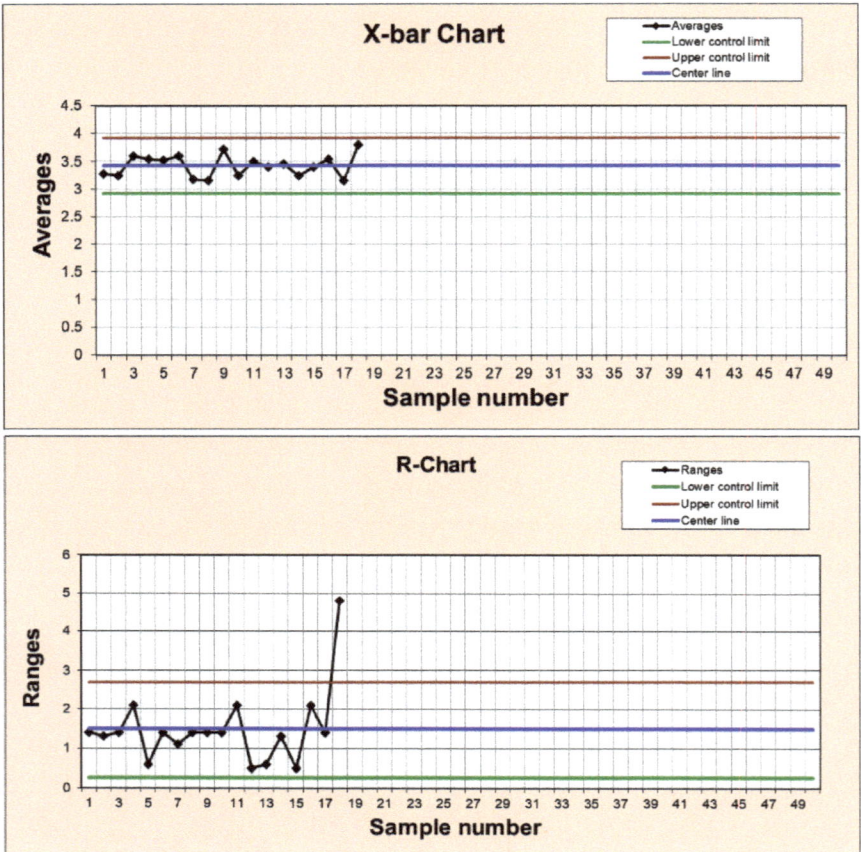

Control chart example – emergency waiting time

In the previous example related to emergency waiting times, we can see that the average waiting time is in control. However, we have a variation problem on day 18, and we can see the spike on the R-chart.

A control chart can, therefore, help identify trends, cycles, shifts, or outliers in the process that may indicate problems or improvement opportunities. By detecting these signals, a control chart can help prevent defects, reduce waste, improve quality, and maintain consistency in the process output. A control chart can also help assess the capability and stability of a process, as well as the effectiveness of any changes or interventions made to the process.

In this chapter, we covered the first two components of the Innovate and Design step: understanding variation and compensating for variation. The next chapter will further explore variation reduction and innovation.

References

9.1: Lean Six Sigma Companion https://abacusteam.ca/

Achieving Excellence Roadmap

Define and Focus on the Value Provided to the Customer	• Review the teams, structure, team roles • Elevate leadership • Focus on Psychology and change management • Identify quick wins, quick improvements • Implement Agile practices: adaptability, communication, KPIs
Define and Understand How the Value Streams	• Understand and improve the processes • Introduce Short term alignment practices • Introduce value stream mapping
Innovate and Design	• Understand variation • Compensate for variation • Reduce variation: VOC, process mapping, analysis • Learn from the hidden champions
Optimize the Flow	• Work to takt time • Build models for the key processes
Become Demand Focused	• Plan for every request • Introduce Pull • Foster a culture of continuous progress

Total People Involvement   Voice of the Customer, Employees, Partners

113

Chapter 10 – Innovate and Design

Innovate and Design

- Understand variation
- Compensate for variation
- Reduce variation: VOC, process mapping, analysis
- Learn from the hidden champions

In the previous chapter, we explored how to understand and compensate for variation, focusing on coping with it rather than reducing it. Achieving this is quite significant as variation is hard to manage. In this chapter, we will discuss reducing or eradicating this variation through various techniques, including innovation.

Reducing Complexity in Processes

As discussed in previous chapters, complexity is not a friend. The more complex and the more steps there are in a process, the more defects and variations we can get. A very well-known example is emergency care in Canada. The process for a patient to reach the hospital, register, undergo pre-triage and triage, complete exams, and navigate various lab tests and follow-ups result in long lead times for treatment and significant variability in treatment success. Doctors and nurses must collect multiple pieces of information, which can lead to differing opinions and approaches to treatment.

Going through process mapping, Muda identification, and Muda reduction would reduce this variation. An exercise we led in urgent asthma cases showed recovery time between 24 hours and 10 days. Mapping the process with doctors and nurses helped identify the inefficiencies, reducing the diagnosis steps from forty-seven to twelve and enabling quicker delivery of the right treatments and medications. This resulted in getting a recovery time between 24 hours and 5 days. Still long, but half the time for some patients.

We can observe a significant relationship between the amount of Muda in a process and the amount of variation (Mura).

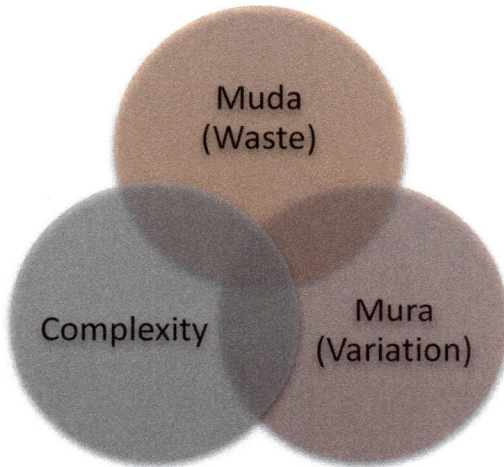

Muda, Mura, Complexity

Root Cause Analysis

Referring to chapter 8, we explored brainstorming, affinity diagrams, fishbones, Five Whys, process mapping, and data collection. These tools should be applied sequentially in this phase to identify the causes of variation.

Below, you will find a summary of the root cause analysis steps covered.

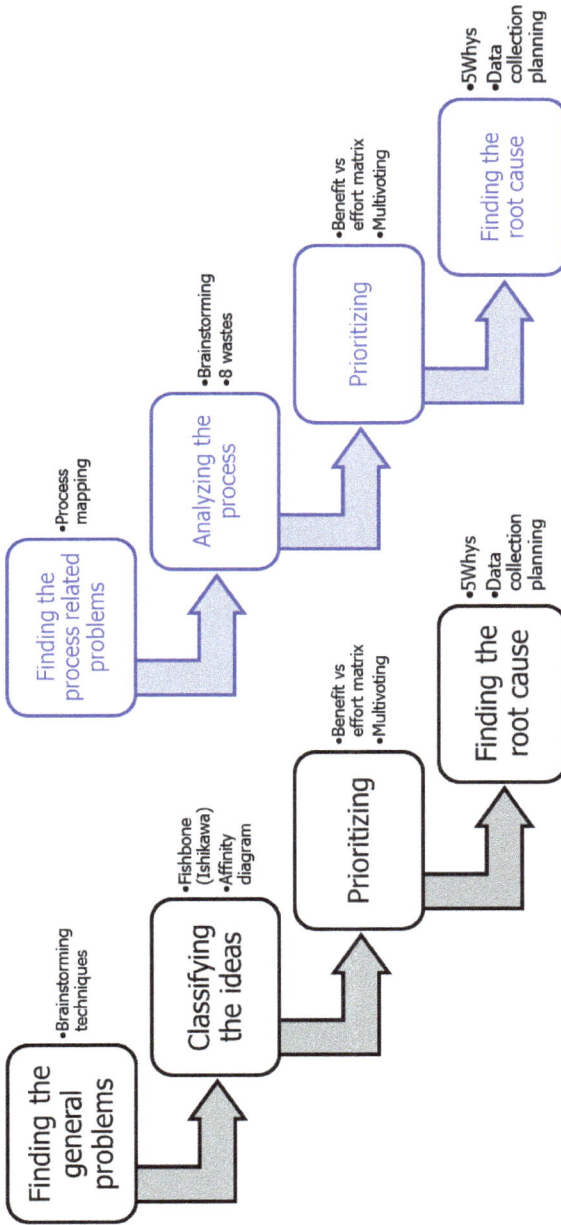

Root Cause Analysis Steps

116

Later in this book, we will introduce more advanced concepts, such as modelling, statistical regression, and machine learning. It is important not to skip steps, as it is crucial to have the team, employees, and managers fully on board.

Comparing Methods

In the previous chapter, we presented an example of patients waiting in an emergency room. The boxplot below shows data from 2018 to 2019, during which changes were made to the admission and triage processes. We explained the t-test and its use in comparing averages, determining that the 2019 process is, on average, better than the 2018 process. Additionally, we can compare the variations to see which method is more consistent.

To do this, we will be using the F-test. The lower the p-value, the more confident we are that the difference is real and not due to random variation. We typically look for p-values lower than 0.05 (5%).

In the example that was built with the Lean Six Sigma Companion (10.1), the p-value is 0.005. Therefore, we can be confident that there is a significant difference in the variance. The variance is the square of the standard deviation.

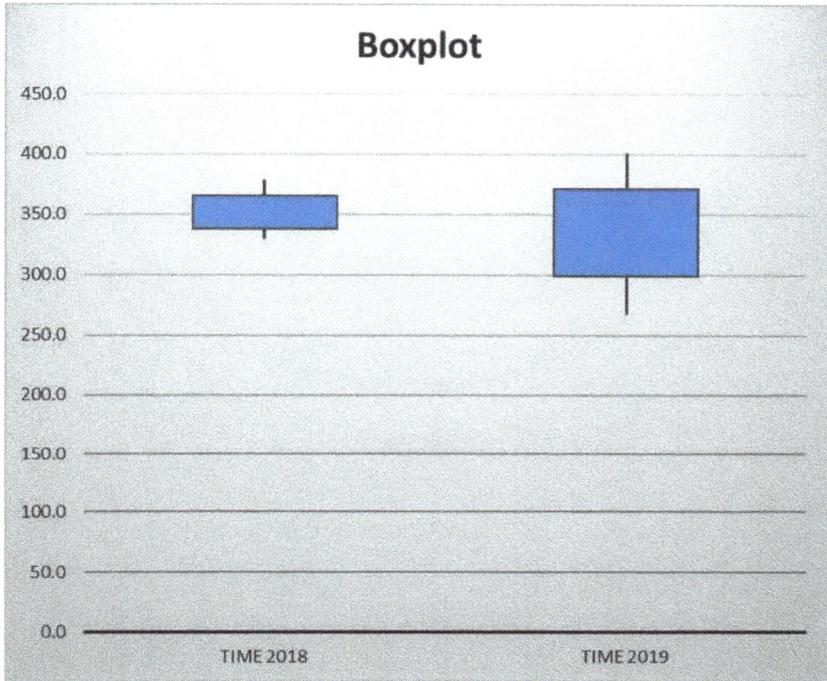

Boxplot

F-Test or Test for Equal Variance

F-test	0.005

There is a significant difference if result is lower than 0.05

Boxplot comparing the 2018 method to the 2019 method *and* **F-test**

The results below show that the new variation is twice as large as it was in 2018. This is an intriguing situation: while the average patient experiences a reduced wait time, some may wait longer due to increased variation. Although the 2019 process is an improvement, we still need to review and refine it to reduce this variation.

This illustrates the ability to evaluate different methods or processes and determine which ones should be prioritized.

Confidence Intervals and statistics

	Time 2018	Time 2019
Alpha	0.05	0.05
n samples	29	29
Average	351.80	331.09
Std dev	21.40	44.01
CI	8.1	16.7
Lower CI	343.7	314.3
Upper CI	359.9	347.8

2018 and 2019 comparison

Poka Yoke – Error Proofing

Poka Yoke is a Japanese term that means "mistake-proofing" or "error prevention". It is an improvement technique designed to eliminate defects or errors in products or processes by making it impossible or exceedingly difficult to make mistakes, thereby also reducing variation. Poka Yoke can be applied to any type of process, whether it is manufacturing, service, or office.

Some examples of Poka Yoke in manufacturing processes are:

- Using jigs or fixtures that only allow the parts to be assembled in the correct orientation or position.
- Using sensors or detectors that measure and control the temperature, pressure, or speed of a machine or process.
- Using devices or mechanisms that prevent the operator from starting the machine or process until all the safety checks or preconditions are met.

In transactional or office-related processes:

- Using checklists or standard operating procedures to ensure that all the steps of a process are followed correctly and nothing is missed.

- Using barcodes or QR codes to scan and verify the identity and status of a product, customer, or document.
- Using automated software or systems that prevent duplicate entries, incorrect data, or unauthorized transactions.
- Using colour-coded labels, signs, or buttons to indicate the correct choice or action for a given situation.
- Using alarms, alerts, or feedback mechanisms to notify the user of any errors, deviations, or anomalies in the process.
- Using templates or forms that have predefined fields, formats, or validations to ensure that the information entered is complete, consistent, and accurate.
- Using electronic signatures or passwords to authenticate and authorize the sender and receiver of a document or message.
- Using locks, keys, or codes to secure and access cabinets, drawers, or rooms that contain confidential or sensitive information or materials.

The more Poka Yoke we have in a process, the less inspection we need to take care of, which is also a time and cost-benefit.

Learning From Hidden Champions

Hidden champions, or lead users, are firms or individuals that innovate ahead of the market and create solutions for their own needs, often without being aware of their potential value for others. They are a valuable source of ideas and feedback for other innovators, as they have a deep understanding of the problems and the context in which they occur. Let us cover some examples of hidden champions or lead users.

3M invented the Post-It notes, the Scotch tape, and many other products by allowing its employees to spend 15% of their time on their own projects. This practice is ground-breaking because it allows employees to dedicate time outside of their assigned activities and projects.

Cummins reclaims truck engines it sells and remanufactures them into brand-new engines rather than starting from scratch each time. This creates a win-win situation for the customers who need to buy expensive engines and Cummins, who can optimize their flow of material and resources. Here, we can also see the added benefit of remanufacturing products instead of simply discarding or recycling them. This allows us to retain most of the added value rather than disposing of it. By studying remanufacturing practices from the company, we aim not to replicate their methods but to draw inspiration from them.

Patagonia offers clothes repair services on what was sold to extend the life of the products they sold. Here again, customers can keep their beloved clothing for much longer and spend less money. For Patagonia, this ensures the loyalty of customers by enhancing their reputation and trust in the brand.

Some restaurants allow you to customize your own salads, pizzas, or pasta dishes from a set of options. This concept opens up numerous possibilities for configuring furniture pieces, laptops, or insurance policies.

A few years ago in Montreal, Canada, I discovered a clothing store that transformed into a nightclub at night. They managed to switch over in just 30 minutes without any visible damage, spills or lingering smells by morning.

How do we identify hidden champions? We need to define the domain or problem area in which we are interested.

We can then conduct a web search or hire consultants to find existing examples of successful solutions, innovations, or best practices in the domain or problem area. It is important to involve key employees in this process. It will be a learning experience as well to develop new hidden champions.

It is possible to contact the creators, providers, or users of the examples and ask them about their motivations, needs, challenges, and experiences. Try to understand how they produced their solutions, how they use or implement them, and what benefits or value they derive from them. Then, we synthesize the findings and generate insights, recommendations, or lessons learned from the examples.

In this chapter, we covered the last two aspects of the Innovate and Design step: reducing variation and learning from hidden champions. At this point, it's important to emphasize the significance of proceeding step by step!

References

10.1: Lean Six Sigma Companion https://abacusteam.ca/

Achieving Excellence Roadmap

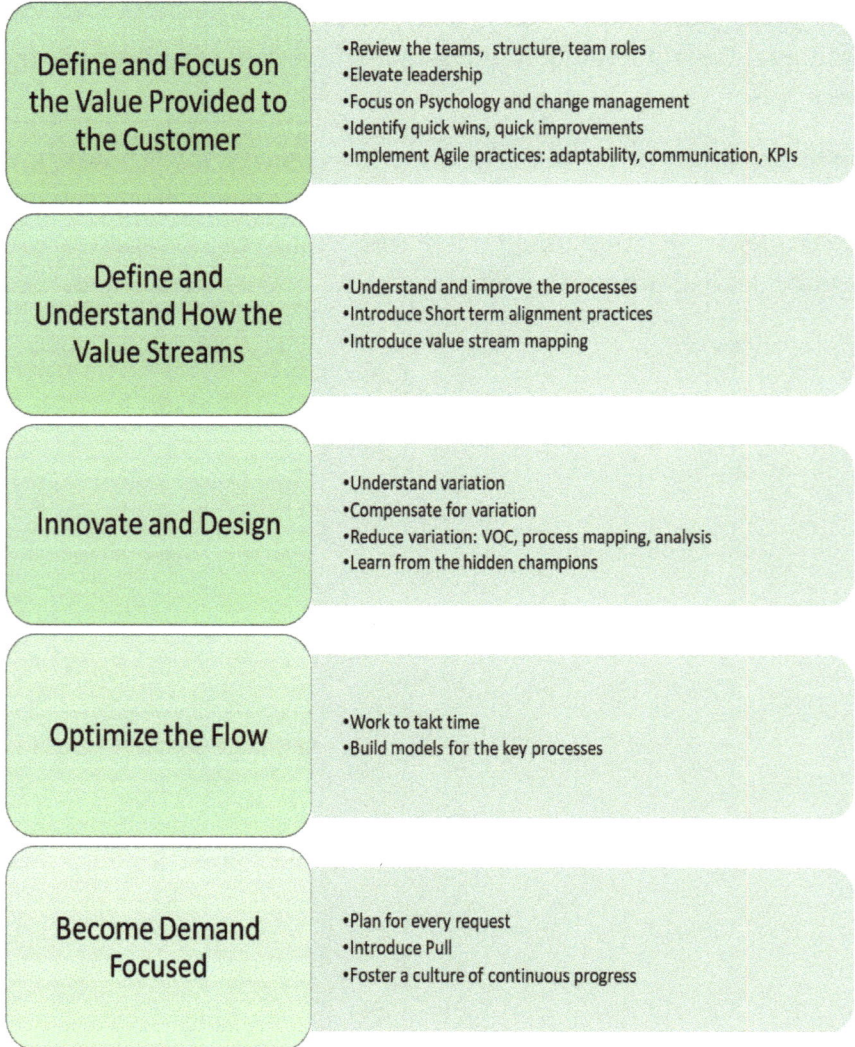

Define and Focus on the Value Provided to the Customer

- Review the teams, structure, team roles
- Elevate leadership
- Focus on Psychology and change management
- Identify quick wins, quick improvements
- Implement Agile practices: adaptability, communication, KPIs

Define and Understand How the Value Streams

- Understand and improve the processes
- Introduce Short term alignment practices
- Introduce value stream mapping

Innovate and Design

- Understand variation
- Compensate for variation
- Reduce variation: VOC, process mapping, analysis
- Learn from the hidden champions

Optimize the Flow

- Work to takt time
- Build models for the key processes

Become Demand Focused

- Plan for every request
- Introduce Pull
- Foster a culture of continuous progress

Total People Involvement   Voice of the Customer, Employees, Partners

123

Chapter 11 – Optimize the flow

Optimize the Flow

Work to takt time

Build models for the key processes

Welcome to optimization. In our Achieving Excellence roadmap, we have seen how to define and focus on the value, how to define and understand how the value should stream, and we discussed innovation and design. We have reached a stage where our workflows and processes have matured significantly, reducing waste and variation while simplifying our operations. Many organizations might pause at this point, especially if their products or services are generating substantial revenue. However, true innovation and design go beyond merely generating ideas. They require a deep understanding of how to optimize product and service development flows, ensuring timely delivery of necessary changes and innovations to the market. This is what it means to work to takt time: delivering to customers what they need, when they need it, and understanding the pace at which we must introduce new products or changes. In this section, we will explore the two key components of this roadmap step: what it takes to work to takt time, and how to model and optimize our processes.

What is Takt Time Again?

Takt time is the beat rate at which we need to deliver a product or service to a customer. If customers place 100 calls per day to a call centre, and the call centre operates for 8 hours per day, then the takt time is 8 hours / 100 calls = 4.8 minutes per call. This means that we need to answer a call every 4.8 minutes to meet the customer demand. Otherwise, we will create a backlog.

As seen in chapter 8, we can also develop a value stream map to understand where the bottlenecks in the process are and on which steps we would need to take action.

	Take order	Prep	Oven	Final prep	Deliver food
	2	4	1	1	1
CT	5	24	17	6	2
SU	0	0	0	0	0
Yield	95%	90%	80%	85%	99%
Batch	2	2	5	1	2

Timeline: 5.0 — 48 — 24 — 3.4 — 17 — 6 — 6 — 1 — 2

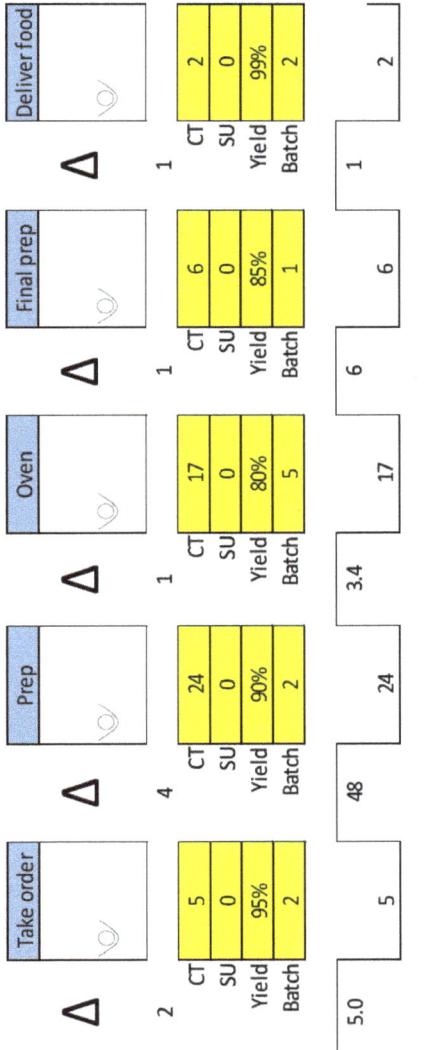

Process time	54
Lead time	117.4
Efficiency	46.0%
Takt time	10

Value Stream Map Example

Monitoring Our Performance versus the Takt Time

Think about the last time that you walked into a Tim Horton's or a Starbucks coffee shop, and if you never did, you should definitively pay a visit. They use visual boards to monitor the performance of their order delivery versus waiting time. As soon as an order does not meet the required takt time, the order is flagged in red or orange for further escalation, where supervisors or other employees jump in to help.

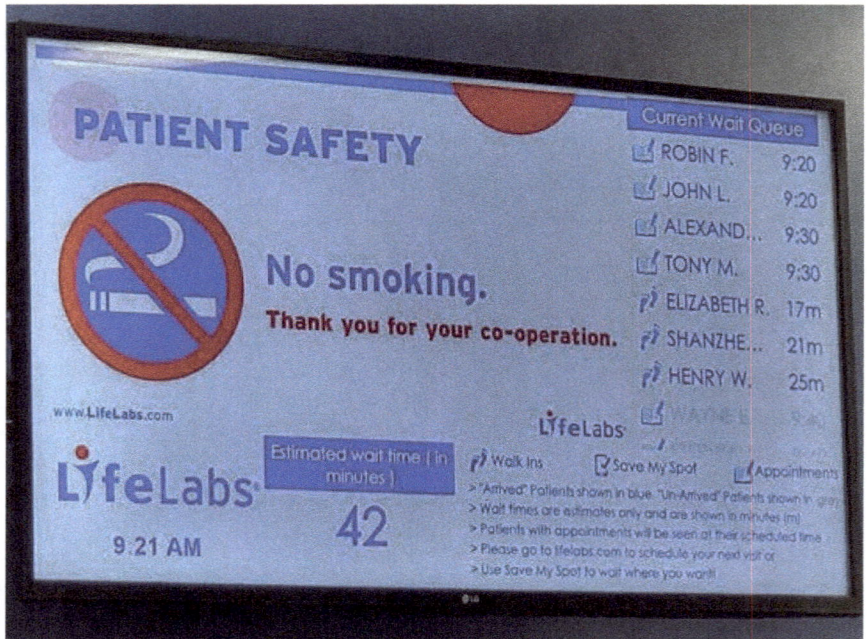

LifeLabs Public Display

In the above example from a Lifelabs Clinic in Ontario, Canada, we can see that the queue is being tracked, which gives useful information to the staff as well as to the patients.

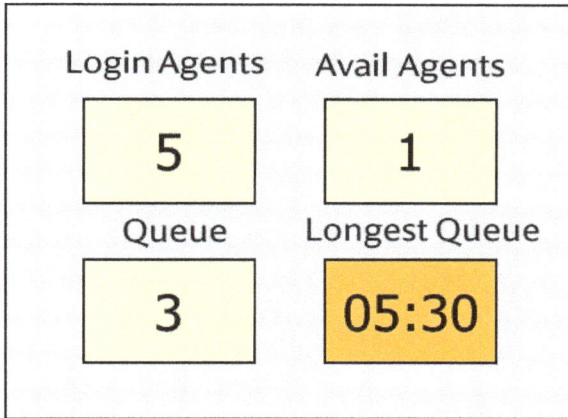

Call Center Tracker

By examining the call centre tracker, we can easily assess our performance using colour-coded responses. For instance, if the longest waiting time is 5 minutes and 30 seconds, colour coding can indicate when escalation or additional support is needed.

Time	Plan	Actual	Status	Notes
8:00 AM	100	100	Green	
9:00 AM	100	95	Orange	*2 orders missing address*
10:00 AM	100	102	Green	
11:00 AM	100	102	Green	
12:00 PM	NA			
1:00 PM	100	101	Green	
2:00 PM	100	100	Green	
3:00 PM	100	94	Orange	*label printer issue*
4:00 PM	50	50	Green	
4:30 PM	NA			

Short Interval Control Board

This example of a short interval control board outlines the planned tasks, such as processing invoices or handling call production, and displays our actual performance in comparison to the plan. We can then flag the discrepancies, take action, and take notes of what were the issues that occurred, as we might wish to take some preventive actions towards those for the next day.

Please note that takt time changes depending on the time of the day, the week, the month or depending on seasonality.

Getting Our Processes to Takt Time

Metrics do change behaviours, and as soon as we are monitoring our process through visual management or control boards, we are sharing with everyone the importance of meeting the expectations of the customer. Nevertheless, the process can still be challenging. Let us share a few methods to ensure that we meet takt time.

Work Balancing and Single Request Flow

Referring to a value stream map, we have already discussed that every step must meet takt time, or beat rate, to prevent delays. Work balancing is the process of distributing the workload across different steps or stations in a process to ensure that each step operates at the same pace and meets the takt time.

Work balancing also enables a single-piece flow, or in other terms, a single request flow. Everyone works on one request or service at a time instead of batching. Batching causes some additional delays as we would need to process a full batch of 200 passports or 200 assemblies. Let us explain what difference it makes. In a bunch production of 200 passports, the first person would process the 200 units, which would take days, and then pass it down to the next person. The next person would do the same, ending up with a process that would take weeks. In a single-piece flow, even if the requests for passports come in exceptionally large quantities, the first person would just process one and pass it down the chain, thus taking a few minutes or a few hours instead of days. The overall result for customers is that the total time would take days instead of weeks.

Batch Flow

Single Piece Flow

Single Piece Flow

Work balancing can have several advantages, such as:

- Reducing waste and inefficiency by eliminating bottlenecks, overproduction, waiting, and inventory.

- Improving flow and throughput by synchronizing the activities and minimizing interruptions or delays.

- Enhancing quality and customer satisfaction by ensuring consistent and timely delivery of products or services that meet the specifications and expectations.

- Increasing flexibility and responsiveness by enabling faster adaptation to changes in demand or requirements.

- Boosting morale and teamwork by creating a smooth and harmonious work environment where everyone contributes and supports each other. People are encouraged to help people around them.

In the example below that comes from a taxation services office, we can see that the work at Step 2 is much longer than the other steps. The Takt Time in this situation was close to 60 minutes. By distributing the work at Step 2 to the steps surrounding it, Step 1 and Step 3, we are getting rid of the bottleneck. Of course, we need to provide training and guidance and make sure that people are ready to help each other.

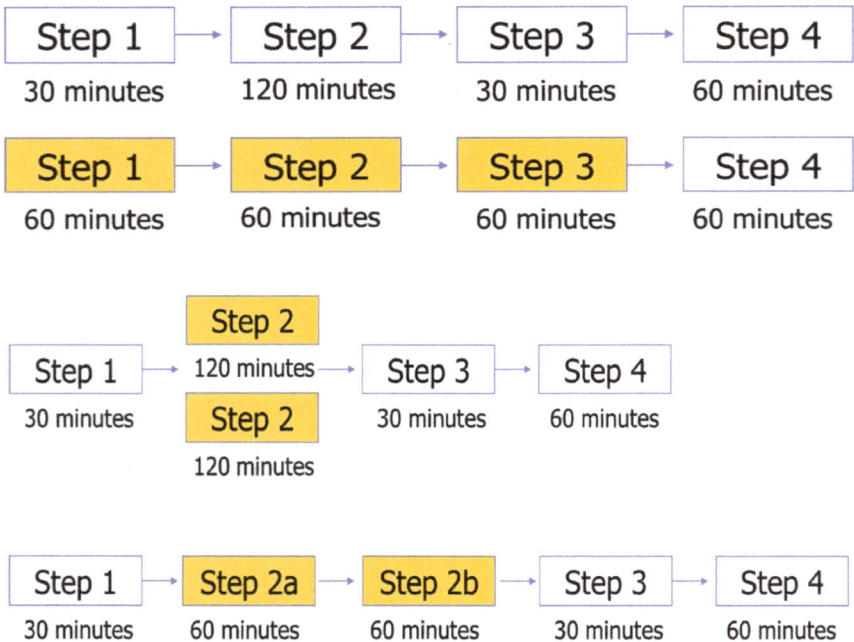

Step 1	Step 2	Step 3	Step 4
30 minutes	120 minutes	30 minutes	60 minutes

Step 1	Step 2	Step 3	Step 4
60 minutes	60 minutes	60 minutes	60 minutes

	Step 2		
Step 1	120 minutes	Step 3	Step 4
30 minutes	Step 2	30 minutes	60 minutes
	120 minutes		

Step 1	Step 2a	Step 2b	Step 3	Step 4
30 minutes	60 minutes	60 minutes	30 minutes	60 minutes

Work Balancing example

Adding Resources

We can, of course, add resources to the process by hiring or moving people from another department. Taking the same example as before, we can add a second desk with another person in Step 2. This can be done in two ways. In the first option, we can double the station, therefore, we would have two tasks being completed every 120 minutes at Step 2. The second option is to distribute the work into two separate desks, which take 60 minutes each. In either case, we would relieve the bottleneck and meet Takt Time.

The downside of this solution is the extra cost that would be incurred, as well as the extra time that it would take to hire.

Process Improvement

Work balancing and adding supplementary resources are good solutions. However it is always recommended to look at the bottleneck for waste and variation reduction. Very often, we neglect to observe and build a process map of the problematic steps as we assume that our current process and the way that we perform provides only value-added.

In the case of the taxation office, employees were spending a considerable time logging into their systems in the morning and looking for information and guidance. These were reduced by simplifying the morning set up and systems logging and ensuring that they had the right information nearby, well identified, located, and labelled.

Modeling the Key Processes

We will discuss the ways to go further into our analysis and refine our response to Takt Time.

So far, we have discussed understanding how well we are doing and our way of working through tools such as value stream mapping, process mapping, and diverse ways to reduce Muda (waste) and Mura (variation). This is the first step of the diagram above, which presents the process modelling options.

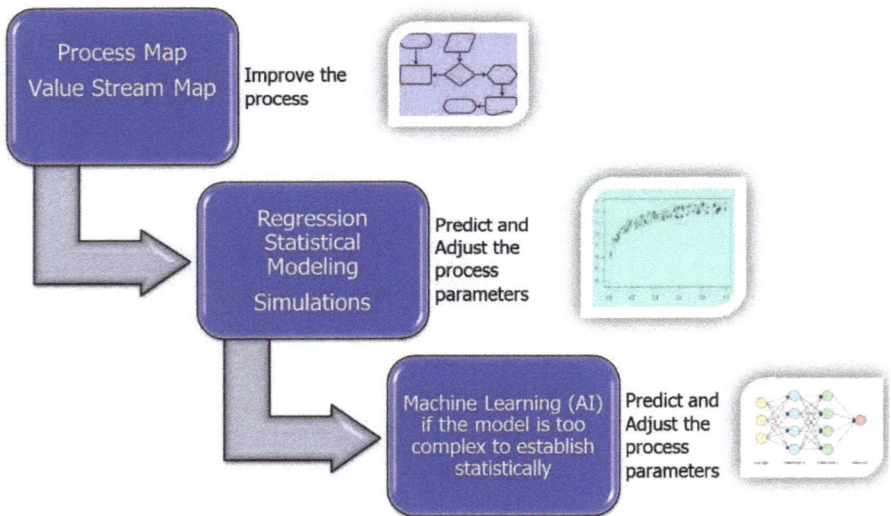

Process modelling options diagram

Regression Statistical Modeling

The next step of the modelling options diagram is to conduct a regression analysis or a simulation.

A regression is a statistical method that examines the relationship between one or more independent variables (factors) and a dependent variable (performance). Regression analysis can help us to identify the causes of variation in our process, to quantify the impact of several factors on our performance, and to predict our future performance based on historical data.

Some of the benefits of regression analysis are:

- It can reveal the causal relationships between factors and performance and help us to understand how changes in one factor affect the other.
- It can measure the strength and direction of the correlation between factors and performance and help us rank the importance of several factors.
- It can generate predictions and forecasts for our performance based on the regression equation and help us to plan and prepare for future scenarios.
- It can support process improvement initiatives by identifying the key drivers of performance, suggesting areas for improvement, and evaluating the effectiveness of interventions.

The example below, created with the free Data Analysis module in Microsoft Excel, illustrates a regression aiming at predicting the length of stay in a hospital-based on data collection on the length of stay and a few potential factors for gastrointestinal troubles. The factors collected are the following:

- Time to see the physician.
- Admission lead time
- Hours on serum
- Time to see a physician.

SUMMARY OUTPUT				
Regression Statistics				
Multiple R	0.809188428			
R Square	0.654785912			
Adjusted R Square	0.599551658			
Standard Error	1.789530155			
Observations	30			
ANOVA				
	df	*SS*	*MS*	*F*
Regression	4	151.8549198	37.96372995	11.85470725
Residual	25	80.06045435	3.202418174	
Total	29	231.9153742		
	Coefficients	*Standard Error*	*t Stat*	*P-value*
Intercept	9.020834091	2.583845786	3.491243223	0.001804685
age	1.011835541	0.272497643	3.713190059	0.001030821
time to see physician	0.020861933	0.550156463	0.037920001	0.970052652
Admission lead time	4.931231381	1.419503688	3.473912342	0.00188476
hours on serum	-0.545462995	0.185027806	-2.948005523	0.006839185

Regression analysis example

R-squared is a measure of how well the regression model fits the data. It is also called the coefficient of determination, and it ranges from 0 to 1. A higher R-squared means that the model explains more of the variation in the data and that the model is more accurate. However, the R-squared does not indicate whether the model is the right one for the data or whether the relationship is causal, as it might be a coincidence. We typically look for an R-squared of 0.64 or higher to say that the model is a particularly good fit.

The adjusted R-squared is a modified version of the R-squared that considers the number of independent variables in the model. The adjusted R-squared is always lower than or equal to the R-squared, and it is more useful for comparing models with different numbers of variables. In our case, we see that it is 0.59, which is not bad as we are close to 0.64.

The P-value indicates whether the chosen factors are significant and if they affect the outcome, in this case, the length of stay. We look for P-values lower than 0.05 (5%), which means that we are at least 95% confident that the factors make a difference. In this case, we see that the age, mission lead time, and hours on serum are significant. The length of time to see a physician does not make a difference. We should, therefore, rerun the regression analysis and remove the length of time to see a physician.

Regression Statistics	
Multiple R	0.809176159
R Square	0.654766056
Adjusted R Square	0.614931371
Standard Error	1.754829152
Observations	30

ANOVA

	df	SS	MS	F
Regression	3	151.850315	50.61677166	16.4370835
Residual	26	80.06505919	3.079425354	
Total	29	231.9153742		

	Coefficients	Standard Error	t Stat	P-value
Intercept	9.042438917	2.471376941	3.658866751	0.00113054
age	1.012944907	0.265669161	3.812805761	0.000760313
Admission lead time	4.927528613	1.388680601	3.548352739	0.00149984
hours on serum	-0.543574005	0.17474038	-3.110752102	0.004490487

Regression analysis example

We now see that all the p-values are below 0.05; therefore, they are all significant. Observe that the adjusted R-squared is a little higher now.

We, therefore, know what makes a difference for these patients. We can take it a step further and even predict what would be the approximate length of stay. This is a particularly important advantage of regression as not only do we know what makes a difference, but we can configure our process the way we wish to obtain the required performance or results.

We can use the coefficients given by Microsoft Excel to build an equation.

Length of Stay = 9.04 + 1.01 Age + 4.93 Admission lead time − 0.54 Hours on serum

In this example that was used, the regression analysis was performed using data that was collected from real patients going through the process. It is also possible to design an experiment and collect data through those created situations to generate a regression model. This is what is called the Design of the Experiment.

Regression and Simulation

We can say that regression analysis is a type of simulation. However, simulations can go much deeper. For example, we can simulate the flow of patients, a flow of products, or phone calls going through a process using a computer simulation. In that fashion, it is possible to simulate months or years of process behaviour. The challenge with these types of simulations is the time they take to develop and refine before being mature enough to be used. Simulations are typically employed for major projects involving multi-million-dollar investments, such as constructing a new airport or designing an aircraft assembly line. These situations often require optimizing numerous parameters, sometimes in the dozens, hundreds, or even thousands. If we take the example of an assembly line, we will need to think about the staffing, materials, tools, the distinct types of wastes that we need to dispose of, information systems, ageing, ventilation, electricity, air, compressed air, safety, and many other factors.

Machine Learning (AI)

The last option of our modelling diagram is related to machine learning, commonly called artificial intelligence. Although we could author a full book on this topic, we will go through an overview of the differences between statistics and regression.

Machine learning is a branch of artificial intelligence that aims to create systems that can learn from data and make predictions or decisions, and we do not need to program them explicitly. Machine learning differs from statistics and regression in several ways. First, machine learning often deals with complex and high-dimensional data that cannot be easily modelled by simple equations or assumptions. This is the main reason we sometimes diverge from statistics to adopt machine learning. Second, machine learning focuses on identifying patterns and generalizations that can be applied to new and unseen data, capturing nonlinear and interactive relationships among variables. Here, we are exploring machine learning in the context of modelling and predicting business processes and performance. It is also widely used for text, image, video, and sound creation and search, as exemplified by ChatGPT for Microsoft Copilot.

Let us go through an example of its application. This is an example based on exploratory research that was aimed at predicting patient discontinuation risks in a pool of 50,000 people. These patients needed to self-inject dosages of medication to alleviate and heal severe cases of arthritis. It is not possible to call every patient every week to ensure that they are OK; the cost of such an operation would be around fifteen billion Canadian dollars per year.

The first step is to thoroughly understand the process, which allows us to then build an effective regression model. You will find below the result of one of these regressions after we removed many of the nonsignificant factors. As we can see, the P-values are all under 0.05. Therefore, all these factors are significant in the model. However, we can see that the R-squared are not particularly good, as they are much lower than our target of 65%. We conducted multiple iterations using these factors and others, including exploring interactions between them. For instance, we examined whether treatment dosage combined with gender creates additional effects that could enhance the model. Below, you will find one of the most effective models we developed, which can be used to predict and contact patients, although the error rate may still be relatively high.

Factor	P-Value
Age in 2024	0.040
Enrolment Date	0.000
Enrollment to 1st injection	0.000
Treatment Period	0.000
Gender	0.036
Province	0.006
Treatment dosage	0.000
R squared	**44.74%**
R squared adjusted	**44.68%**

Patient discontinuation regression analysis

We decided to use a machine learning technique known as Classification and Regression Tree (CART). There are many techniques that can be used, and we are very often limited by the amount of data that is available. For instance, it was not possible in this case to use any type of neural network or deep learning technique as the data was insufficient.

Before explaining the next steps, let us briefly describe what is the classification and regression tree technique. It works by recursively partitioning the data into smaller and smaller subsets based on some criteria, such as the value of a feature or the output of a function. Each subset is then assigned to a leaf node, which represents a class label or a numerical value. The result is a tree-like structure that can be used to make predictions for new data points by following the branches from the root node to the leaf node. The advantage of this technique is that it is relatively easy to interpret and visualize.

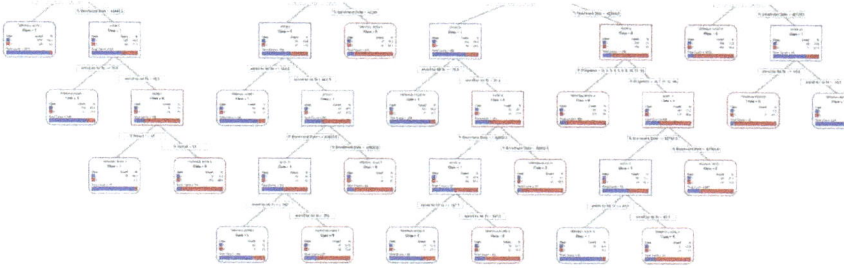

Extract of a CART Tree

Statistics	Training (%)	Test (%)
True positive rate (sensitivity or power)	78.6	78.8
False positive rate (type I error)	4.3	4.2
False negative rate (type II error)	21.4	21.2
True negative rate (specificity)	95.7	95.8

CART result

Above, you will find the results of the tree that was developed after multiple trials and iterations. The training percentages relate to the data that was fed to the model to learn. For example, the true positive rate, indicating our ability to detect discontinuation risk when it exists, stands at 78.6%. Additional statistics related to true and false positives and negatives are also provided. These test percentages reflect new data used to evaluate the model's ability to predict patients at risk of discontinuation. Although the prediction is not perfect, we still have 78.8%, which is much better and much more practical than the result achieved through regression analysis.

This chapter has explored several methods for enhancing our processes. It begins with adhering to the required pace, Takt time, and aligning the development of our products and services accordingly. We also introduced various approaches to advance our processes by gaining a thorough understanding of the key factors influencing them and their relationships.

Achieving Excellence Roadmap

Define and Focus on the Value Provided to the Customer	• Review the teams, structure, team roles • Elevate leadership • Focus on Psychology and change management • Identify quick wins, quick improvements • Implement Agile practices: adaptability, communication, KPIs
Define and Understand How the Value Streams	• Understand and improve the processes • Introduce Short term alignment practices • Introduce value stream mapping
Innovate and Design	• Understand variation • Compensate for variation • Reduce variation: VOC, process mapping, analysis • Learn from the hidden champions
Optimize the Flow	• Work to takt time • Build models for the key processes
Become Demand Focused	• Plan for every request • Introduce Pull • Foster a culture of continuous progress

Total People Involvement   Voice of the Customer, Employees, Partners

Chapter 12 - Become Demand Focused

Become Demand Focused

- Plan for every request
- Introduce Pull
- Foster a culture of continuous progress

We are now at the last maturity level. The organization should now understand its takt time and fluctuations, and the work is balanced. We are optimizing our processes and modelling the key ones to monitor the factors contributing to our success. We are now looking to gain a deeper understanding of demand changes in terms of customization and adaptation. In this chapter, we will first discuss planning for every request. We will then define what is a pull versus a push and how to implement this type of strategy. We will then explore ways to foster continuous progress in performance, growth, and, of course, employee satisfaction.

Plan for Every Request

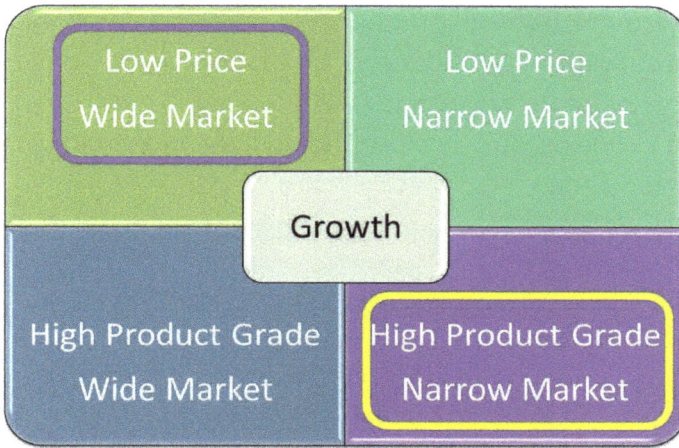

Low Price Wide Market	Low Price Narrow Market
Growth	
High Product Grade Wide Market	High Product Grade Narrow Market

Marketing Strategy

We have already discussed targeting high-end products and services for a niche market, as well as the alternative of focusing on low-priced products and services for a broader market. In all cases, as the organization grows, a need for customization arises. As a customer, I seek customized information from my IT outsourcing suppliers. I would like more predictive insights regarding my company's financial health. Additionally, I want specific home screens and apps tailored for my smartphone and laptop.

The answer to these customers might be no. In the short term, this could make sense, but it could also open the market to innovative disruptors. As an example, Spotify disrupted the music industry by offering online access to millions of songs and podcasts for a monthly fee, as well as personalized playlists and recommendations. Another well-known example is Uber, which disrupted the taxi and transportation industry by connecting drivers and riders through their mobile app for cars and boats. They are now offering assorted options such as ridesharing, food delivery, car and bike rentals.

Therefore, we need to establish the organization's plan to accept or refuse these upcoming requests gradually. People, processes, tools, and systems would need to be improved or redesigned accordingly. Before we decide how to respond to these requests, we need to understand how they relate to our current strategy and value proposition.

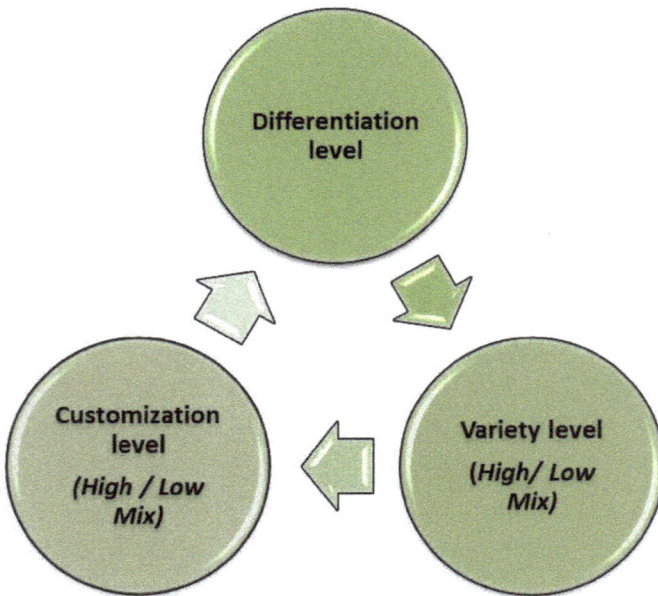

Plan for every request choices

Differentiation, variety, and customization are three concepts that relate to how a product or service can meet the needs and preferences of different customers.

Differentiation involves creating a unique value proposition for a product or service that sets it apart from competitors and appeals to a specific market segment. This concept, which was discussed earlier in this book, is always essential. As an example of effective differentiation, Bulldog shaving products stand out. While they may appear similar to other products on the market, Bulldog's branding emphasizes ecological awareness by using materials like bamboo instead of plastic.

Variety refers to offering a range of options or features for a product or service that cater to different tastes and preferences. For example, Starbucks offers its customers a variety of coffee drinks, flavours, and sizes. For software such as TurboTax, different standard options can be purchased.

Customization refers to tailoring a product or service to the individual needs and desires of each customer, often by involving them in the design or delivery process. For example, Nike allows customers to customize their own shoes by choosing the colour, style, and materials. In 2024, GE Appliance announced that it would involve its customers in the design process to offer custom looks. ERP (Enterprise Resource Planning) software providers can develop custom functions and reports for their customers. For example, Dell offers mass customization and has developed its systems and processes, from order entry to delivery, to cater to these needs. Their focus is on reducing Muda at each step while trying to keep the capital investments to a minimum.

This is the reason we are discussing these at this stage of the roadmap, as without optimized processes, it might be highly costly to achieve any level of variety or customization with unstable processes. On our roadmap, a key element to make this happen is the concept of 'pull.'

Pull

A push delivery system is one in which products or services are produced or delivered in advance based on forecasts or schedules and then sold or provided to customers. Push delivery systems tend to have high inventory levels, low responsiveness, and high waste, as they often result in overproduction or underproduction of products or services that may not match what customers want or need.

In the example below, we are asking our suppliers to send us one box per week, whether we need it or not. In this case, if we do not sell, we are building inventory week after week. If we sold more than expected, there would be no adjustments in our supply orders, leading to stock shortages and missed sales opportunities.

Push – Follow the plan

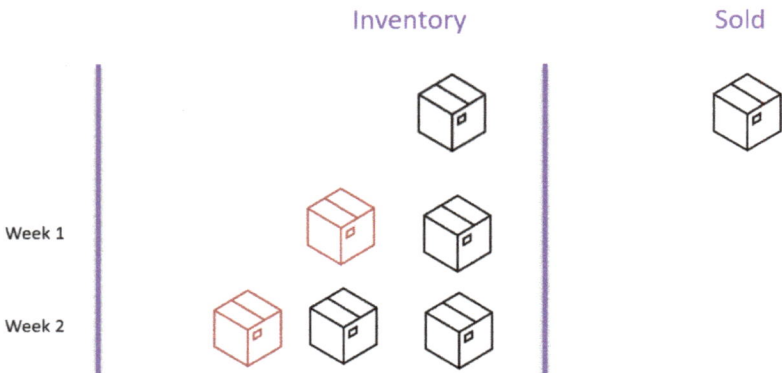

Push delivery system

A pull delivery system (1) is one in which products or services are produced or delivered on demand based on the actual needs or orders of customers. The difference between push and pull delivery systems is related to the timing and quantity of production or delivery, as well as the degree of alignment with customer preferences. Pull delivery systems tend to have low inventory levels, high responsiveness, and low waste, as they aim to produce or deliver only what is needed when it is needed and in the right amount. Pull delivery systems are more customer-oriented and flexible, but they also require more coordination and communication among the various parts of the processes.

As we can see below, we send a signal or a request to a supplier only when we need to. We will also request more if we need more. This type of signal can be electronic, such as a purchase order or an online request, or it could be a physical ticket. A pull system is also referred to as Kanban or "just in time." In situations where this does not work, people refer to it as "just too late." Very often, the reason for failure is the lack of consistency of the processes. It would be exceedingly difficult to implement a pull system on a process that is full of waste and variation.

Pull – Adjust to the demand

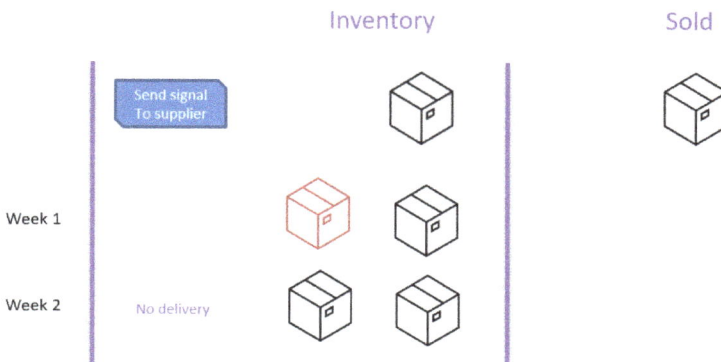

Pull delivery system

In service environments such as projects, healthcare, or information technologies, it is common to find a visual management tool referred to as a Kanban Board (2).

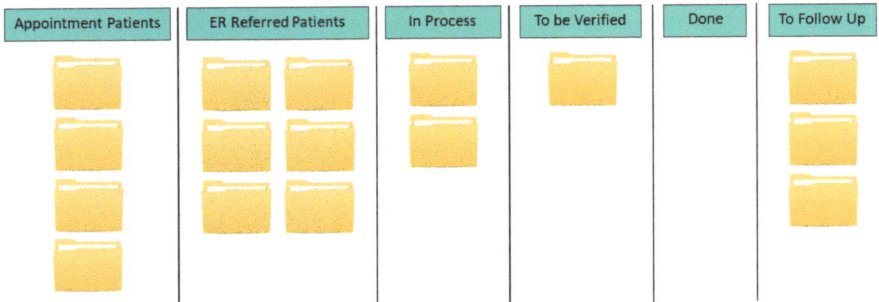

| Appointment Patients | ER Referred Patients | In Process | To be Verified | Done | To Follow Up |

Kanban board example

In this example, only two patients are currently in process, as we only have the capacity to see two at the time. Bringing in more patients to overcrowd the examination rooms or leaving them in the corridors would be both useless and very confusing. Once we are done with one of the two patients, then we can take the next one from the column on the left. This type of board can be applied to any type of task that needs to be performed.

Kanban for Material Goods

In environments where physical replenishment is necessary – such as for merchandise, manufacturing parts, supplies, medication, and food – a calculation is used to determine the required safety level. This ensures we do not run out of stock while still having enough to meet demand.

The kanban number 'N' is the number of containers or cards that circulate between the supplier and the demanding process. It indicates how many units of work are in progress at any given time.

In the example below, we calculated a Kanban of three. We could represent it by showing that we have one container on site ready to be used, one signal sent to the supplier to start working on a new delivery, and one container that was previously requested, which is in transit and should arrive soon. Therefore, there is a total of three at any time. The maximum that we would get if we did not use the inventory is three containers.

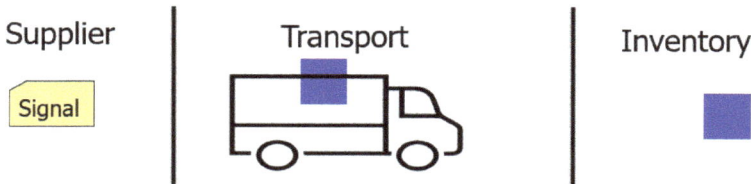

Example with a kanban number N of three

One equation for defining the number of kanban (Kanban quantity) is (3):

$$N = D * L * SF / Q$$

Where D is the average daily usage based on history and forecasts, L is the lead time to get the goods once we request them, SF is the safety factor, usually set at 1.2, and Q is the container quantity or lot size for each order. The safety factor is typically set at 1.2, which creates a 20% buffer in case demand increases by 20%. Other safety factors can be chosen depending on our risk appetite. The 20% is historically considered a good trade-off between safety and inventory costs.

This equation means that the number of kanbans depends on how much is used per day, how long it takes to replenish, how much buffer is needed to prevent stockouts, and how much is delivered in each container. The higher the usage, lead time, and safety factor, the more kanban are needed. The higher the container quantity, the fewer kanban are needed. This equation helps balance the demand and supply of a process and minimize the inventory holding costs.

Referring to the example of our Kanban of three, the calculation is:

D = 30 per day on average

L = 15 days

SF = 1.2

Q = 200 parts per container

N = D * L* SF / Q = 30 * 15 * 1.2 / 200 = 2.7

Finally, we round it up to three.

Pull - What About the Takt Time of Innovation

We also need to monitor how needs change and how consumers feel about the novelty of our products and services. We might see rising competitive offerings. This brings us back to what we discussed at the beginning of our operational excellence roadmap – making sure that we always link with the customers and their voices.

We can think about Motorola, which invaded the market in the 1990s with its high-quality cell phones and pagers. Motorola ignored the need to optimize and pursue smaller emergent customers. They ignored the emerging trend called the "Internet." Motorola refused to integrate this insignificant opportunity into their smartphones. Meanwhile, Nokia and other companies seized this new reality and created the first Internet-enabled smartphones. Motorola joined the competition much later.

A remarkably similar story can be said about BlackBerry, which neglected the importance of a rising category of customers who wished to have a better user interface through "Apps" and better navigation on their phones. When the first iPhone was released in

2007, it offered something different and easier. Blackberry was not the only company affected. LG, HTC, and Motorola already had phones with touch screens. The iPhone was not the first touchscreen device to hit the market, but it was significantly better than the others in terms of its interface and usability.

Therefore, we need to understand the takt time for change and innovation—how quickly customers expect changes to occur. An app or software such as QuickBooks, Microsoft Office, or ChatGPT can be changed on a quarterly or more frequent basis. For the examples given before, such as smartphones, it could be done on a quarterly or yearly basis.

Fostering a Culture of Continuous Progress

We have reflected on and provided several examples highlighting the need to progress step by step and engage people not as passive passengers but as active co-drivers on the journey to operational excellence. In this section, we will discuss key approaches to implement at this stage.

Continuous People Development

Learning by doing, training, and coaching are an integral part of all the steps we have discussed. We need to make sure that on top of the business activities and improvements; there is a regular reflection on the personal development of our employees. An annual performance evaluation is just one aspect of this process, albeit an important one, as it facilitates self-reflection for employees and fosters a discussion with their managers. It is also typically tied to career development and succession planning. Managers should also consider which soft skills and technical skills team members need to develop to advance. Some questions to ask to plan training related to the future needs of the organization and the future needs and aspirations of employees are:

- What are the strategic objectives and priorities of the organization for the next year, three years, and five years?
- What are the current and expected gaps in the skills, knowledge, and competencies of the workforce to achieve those objectives and priorities?
- What are the individual career goals and aspirations of the employees, and how do they align with the organizational vision and mission?
- What are the preferred learning styles and preferences of the employees, and how can they be accommodated in the training design and delivery?
- What are the available resources and constraints for training, such as budget, time, space, technology, and trainers?

The answers related to these questions are partly through training through different formats, direct involvement in specific activities or projects, and coaching.

Keeping the Pace Through DMS

Let us expand on the principle of the daily or weekly huddle and discuss the daily management system, or DMS (4). It provides a structure to ensure that performance and quality of execution are achieved.

The first element of a DMS is leader standard work. The key activities that must be performed, whether daily, weekly, or monthly, are identified. They all link to key business processes and customer or patient satisfaction. A documented process must exist for all key activities. After the leader's standard work is created, a routine is established to ensure that it is followed, which reduces surprises and ensures that abnormalities are detected easily and quickly.

Role	Leader standard work (key activities) examples
Project Manager	Cost tracking Schedule Tracking On time tasks completion
IT Manager	Production and sales systems uptime Critical open requests escalation New projects review
Sales Manager	Sales forecast Bookings review Leads review
Production Manager	Daily schedule On time delivery Unresolved quality and production issues review

Leader standard work examples

The second element, visual controls, ensures an immediate understanding of whether a situation is normal. These controls can be as simple as putting tape on the floor to show how many patient beds should be in an intensive care unit or how many carts of finished goods should be in a production area. We have already explored visual management in depth.

In these situations, delimitation with colour or a line is an obvious and straightforward way to assess with objective criteria whether a situation is normal or not. The same type of visual control can be extended in any office or operational environment to monitor the execution of the leader's standard work. Here is an example of such visual control. At the beginning of the week, all cards are turned to display the red side. As the activities are executed, the employees accountable for the activities, including management, turn their cards to the green side. The entire team can see in an instant whether the situation is normal. This may seem like a simple, insignificant example, but when this method is deployed to every function of an organization, the result is seamless visual management of all key activities.

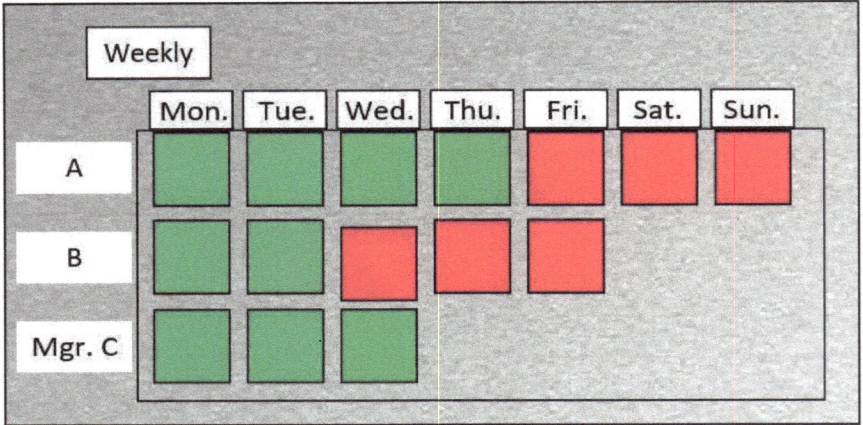

Visual management example

Visual management can create awareness and identify and prevent situations in which an action must be taken. Linking these visuals to leader standard work is an efficient way to track them to closure.

Third, the element that binds these practices together is the daily accountability process. It ties levels and functions together and creates a communication highway.

Consider Triton Electronik. The organization provides design services, prototyping, and short-run production for critical systems such as 911 systems, medical diagnosis equipment, telecommunication base stations, and control modules for trains and subway cars, among other products. The organization's daily accountability model includes diverse levels of communication connected through visual management and focused on the key elements of the leader's standard work. Each function of the organization holds an accountability meeting, called the Tier I meeting, at the beginning of every shift. The target duration of the meeting is five minutes, during which the supervisor reviews the performance from the previous day and listens to the problems or issues that employees foresee for the upcoming day or week. These

155

meetings take place in front of a visual board. The visual control ensures that the leader's standard work elements are performed, key performance indicators (KPI) are reviewed, and new actions are written down. The KPIs focus on quality, on-time delivery, and productivity, with each action assigned a deadline and an owner. After the Tier I meetings, supervisors review the visual boards with the team leads and note any action that requires their involvement. This information also is used as input for the sales and operations planning meeting. A second accountability meeting, the Tier II meeting, occurs in the afternoon between shifts. This meeting is facilitated by the site director and involves all functional directors or managers. The target duration is 15 minutes, during which the site director reviews performance through KPIs, identifies risks and issues, and reviews open key issues.

Certain organizations, such as the Marriott hotels and Pratt and Whitney, have been known to have a structured daily management system going from every department up to the CEO (5).

Tier I meeting—per function
- When: Shift start
- Length: 5 minutes
- Who: Team leader and crew
- Why: Give feedback to crew

Night shift and day shift

Supervisors review the Tier I information and concerns before the planning meeting.

Tier II board is updated: metrics and actions that need director-level support.

Planning meeting
- Review new and ongoing orders, constraints and problems from Tier I meetings.

Tier II meeting—site
- When: 1 p.m.
- Length: 15 minutes
- Who: Site director and directors. Production, supply chain, quality, HR, sales, IT, supervisors and planners, as needed
- Why: Feedback, priorities of the day

Daily accountability

A DMS was implemented at Triton Electronik at a time of accelerated expansion of technologies and manufacturing processes. The DMS helped set the pace for introducing changes and ensuring that key activities were executed and every employee was involved. The ongoing transformation was successful, with a continuous focus on customer quality and delivery. The KPIs showed regular improvement and a reduction in defects.

Unfortunately, a few months after the DMS was implemented and the significant expansion and acquisition activities were completed, Triton Electronik went into bankruptcy protection status because of cash flow problems. Employees had to keep delivering quality products and services to customers for months at an organization with an uncertain future. The organization decided to keep the DMS in place and find out how it would help the employees adapt to the new work environment. Within a few days of the bankruptcy protection announcement, employees progressed from denial to indifference. Through the DMS, a constant communication link was already in place. Employees could express themselves and were heard by management. Ongoing news about the organization's future was also communicated to them with high frequency. The relationship between the organization's success and product and service quality and delivery was clear to everyone. Quality and delivery levels continued to progress. Some recurrent concerns were raised in a Tier I meeting related to résumé preparation coaching and job fairs in case employees lost their jobs. These concerns were brought up at the Tier II meeting as actions and feedback about the arrangement were communicated to employees. When the organization's closure was announced with four months' notice, job fairs and résumé coaching sessions were unveiled at the same time, which was a relief for many employees and a sign of the next steps ahead for their careers. Proactive issues, such as upcoming customer requests, were raised by employees in the Tier I meeting.

Many employees volunteered to help at their level, and preventive measures were taken by many employees who volunteered to help. From the day Triton Electronik's closure was announced to the day it closed, on-time deliveries improved by 18% and quality improved by 23%.

Long-Term Alignment

A full alignment and understanding of the vision and strategy by all employees is what we are aiming for in this part. In common strategic planning activities, senior management produces a strategy and high-level action plans without consulting the different layers of the organization. We will introduce the tool called the Hoshin Kanri, which was developed to create that better alignment.

Hoshin Kanri (6) is a Japanese term that means "the compass that shows the trail to take". It is a strategic planning method that aims to align the vision, goals, and actions of an organization at all levels, from top management to frontline workers. Hoshin Kanri helps organizations focus on the most important objectives, communicate them clearly, and monitor the progress and results.

Hoshin Kanri involves a cyclical process of planning, execution, review, and improvement. We start by developing a long-term vision and strategic goals for the organization. We then break it down into annual objectives and KPIs. We then flow it down and ask each level of the organization for their help, translating the objectives into specific actions and targets for each department, team, and individual. This way, everyone understands how their individual objectives and projects are linked to the overall strategy. We then review the results every second week or every month to identify gaps and create recovery plans.

Hoshin Kanri principle

You will find below an example of the Hoshin Kanri working matrix. Please note that the results are often presented in a simpler representation to the employees. In the example, the strategic directions are identified by the president; then, the vice presidents identify initiatives that connect to them. The black and white dots represent the relationships of these initiatives – black represents a strong link, and white represents a medium strong link. Then, the vice presidents ask directors and managers to produce projects. Finally, everyone comes out with tasks. We can drill down further if we need more detailed granularity.

Hoshin Kanri X-Matrix (working tool)

Initiatives (top)

Initiative	Cumulative progress	Score – Lower Linkage
Address demand for social services, gaps in services, and growing disparities. Sponsor: Arielle Mayer	64%	3.5
Identify and implement innovative and EDIA service delivery models. Sponsor: Giovanna Magana	67%	1.5

Strategic Directions (left)

Strategy number	Strategic Direction	Cumulative progress	Score – Lower Linkage
1	Increase outreach strategies to raise public awareness about social services	65%	1.5
2	Develop strategies to enhance the financial sustainability of social services.	70%	1
3	Invest in staff development and retention strategies to attract a skilled and diverse workforce	68%	1.5

Projects

Project	Timing	Project Number	Departments	Business Unit	Cumulative progress	Status	Score – Lower Linkage
Digitization of client files. Metric: Time to access info cut by 90%. Leader: Rhoda Report	Q1 2025	1	IT	USA Division	75%	On target	1
Funding for palliative care. Metric: Increase funding by 10%. Sponsor: Daniel Carson	Q1 2025	2	Finance	Canada Division	46%	Not meeting target	1.5
Expanding service locations. Metric: 1 new service location per 2 quarters. Sponsor: Noel Scott	Q1 2025	3	Operations	Canada Division	58%	On target	2
Training, mentorship, and professional development opportunities	Q2 2025	4	HR	USA Division	88%	Near target	1.5
Workplace wellness program. Metric: Staff participation rate of 70%. Sponsor: Francesca Stevenson	Q2 2025	5	HR	Canada Division	64%	On target	3

Tasks

Tasks	Tasks Progress	Status (Score Lower Linkage→ / Status↓)	Project Number
File2scan workshop. Metric: Time to access info cut by 90%. Leader: Rob Gerling	75%	Not meeting target	
Location expansion funding plan. Metric: 1 new service location per 2 quarters. Leader: Ronda Bisby	62%	Near target	

Hoshin Kanri working tool example

Hoshin Kanri helps organizations achieve several benefits, such as aligning the vision, goals, and actions of the organization across all levels and ensuring everyone is working towards the same direction. Employees are engaged in the strategic planning process and empowered to take ownership and responsibility for their work. It improves communication and collaboration among different departments, teams, and individuals.

It is a wonderful way of enhancing the efficiency and effectiveness of the organization by eliminating waste, redundancy, and inconsistency and fostering a culture of continuous improvement and learning by encouraging feedback, reflection, and innovation.

A Glimpse at the Future of Business: Linear vs Circular Economy

In this overall demand flow and demand-focused transformation, one trend that we will see becoming more present in the next few years is the transition to a circular economy. It is already a dominant trend in Europe and forcing many companies to comply with certain design choices and practices.

A linear economy is based on the principle of "take, make, dispose", where resources are extracted, transformed into products, and discarded after use. This model creates a lot of waste and pollution and depletes natural resources. For example, most plastic packaging is used only once and then thrown away, ending up in landfills or oceans.

A recycling economy, or a sustainable economy, is an improvement over the linear economy, as it tries to recover some of the materials and energy from the waste stream and reuse them for new products. Recycling reduces the demand for virgin resources and lowers the environmental impact of production and consumption. However, recycling still involves some losses and inefficiencies and does not address the root causes of overconsumption and waste generation. For example, recycling paper saves trees but also consumes water and energy and produces emissions and sludge.

A circular economy (7) is a more radical and systemic shift from the linear economy, as it aims to design out waste and pollution, keep products and materials in use, and regenerate natural systems. A circular economy is based on the principles of reduction by design, reuse, redistribute, repair, maintain, refurbishment, regenerate, or remanufacturing. It promotes the use of renewable energy, biodegradable materials, and closed-loop cycles. It also encourages the adoption of new business models, such as product-as-a-service, sharing platforms, and performance-based contracts.

For example, a circular economy would enable a car manufacturer or appliance to lease its vehicles instead of selling them and provide maintenance and repair services to extend their lifespan while using recycled and renewable materials for their components. The Bundles company serves as a prime example in the appliances business. It offers a product-as-a-service model for household appliances, such as washing machines, dryers, and dishwashers. Instead of selling the appliances, Bundles leases them to its customers and charges them based on their usage. The customers also receive free installation, maintenance, and repair services from Bundles, as well as tips and feedback on how to optimize their energy and water consumption. Bundles use high-quality appliances that are designed to last longer and use fewer resources. It also recovers the appliances at the end of their lease and refurbishes or recycles them for reuse. By doing so, Bundles reduces the environmental impact of appliance production and disposal while providing a convenient and affordable service for its customers. Bundles also creates a closer relationship with its customers and suppliers, as it collects data on the performance and usage of the appliances and shares it with them. This allows Bundles to improve its service quality, customer satisfaction, and resource efficiency while enabling its customers and suppliers to make more informed and sustainable choices.

Another example relates to remanufacturing, which involves restoring used or worn-out products to a like-new condition using original or compatible parts and components. Remanufacturing preserves the value and functionality of the products while reducing material and energy consumption, waste generation, and greenhouse gas emissions compared to producing new ones. Remanufacturing also creates new employment opportunities and enhances customer satisfaction and loyalty. Cummins is a global leader in engine remanufacturing, with over fifty facilities worldwide. Cummins collects used engines from its customers and dismantles them into core components, which are then cleaned, inspected, repaired, or replaced as needed. The remanufactured engines are then reassembled, tested, and certified to meet the same quality and performance standards as new ones. Cummins claims that remanufacturing saves up to 85% of the energy and 90% of the raw materials required for new engine production and reduces CO_2 emissions by up to 80%.

Repairing is another example of the circular economy, as it aims to extend the useful life of products and prevent them from becoming waste. Repairing involves fixing minor damages or malfunctions, such as replacing a broken zipper, mending a tear, or soldering a wire. Repairing reduces the need for new production and consumption and preserves the embodied energy and materials of the products. Repairing also empowers consumers and communities to take care of their belongings and reduce their environmental impact. Patagonia is a well-known example of a company that promotes repair as part of its circular economy strategy. Patagonia is an outdoor clothing and gear brand that advocates for environmental and social responsibility. Patagonia encourages its customers to repair their products instead of discarding them and provides numerous services and resources to facilitate this. For instance, Patagonia offers free repairs for its products at its stores or through its online repair program. Patagonia operates the Worn Wear program, which sells second-hand Patagonia products that have been repaired and restored. Patagonia also educates its customers on how to repair their own products by providing online guides, videos, and workshops. Patagonia claims that repairing can extend the life of a garment by an average of nine years and reduce its carbon footprint by 80%.

As part of the circular economy, recycling comes as the last option as it degrades the value and creates waste.

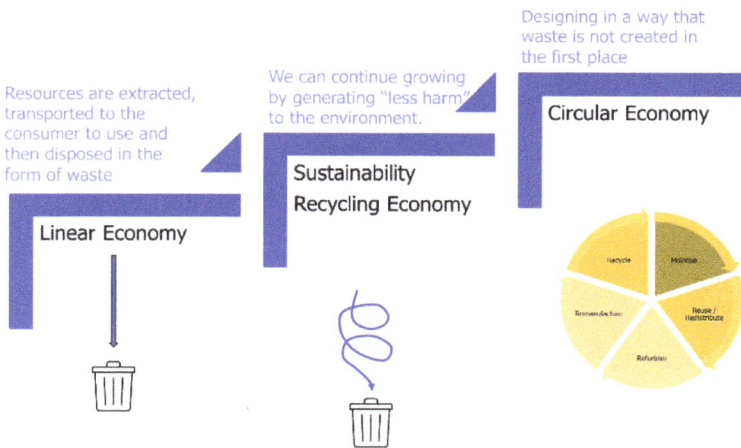

Designing in a way that waste is not created in the first place

Circular Economy

We can continue growing by generating "less harm" to the environment.

Sustainability
Recycling Economy

Resources are extracted, transported to the consumer to use and then disposed in the form of waste

Linear Economy

Recycle   Minimise

Remanufacture   Reuse / Redistribute

Refurbish

Linear, recycling, and circular economy

Becoming demand-focused can introduce a certain level of contradiction in terms of developing more complex processes, generating more waste, and accommodating greater variation. Having a good understanding of our processes allows us to make better choices and continue the journey towards operational excellence.

(1) Lean Thinking, James Womack
(2) Essential Scrum: A Practical Guide to the Most Popular Agile Process Paperback, Kenneth Rubin
(3) Lean Production Simplified: A Plain-Language Guide to the World's Most Powerful Production System, Pascal Dennis
(4) Creating a Lean Culture: Tools to Sustain Lean Conversions, David Mann
(5) Toyota Kata: Managing People for Improvement, Adaptiveness, and Superior Results, Mike Rother
(6) Hoshin Kanri: Policy Deployment for Successful TQM, Yoji Akao
(7) The Circular Economy: A Wealth of Flows, Ken Webster, Ellen MacArthur

Achieving Excellence Roadmap

Define and Focus on the Value Provided to the Customer

- Review the teams, structure, team roles
- Elevate leadership
- Focus on Psychology and change management
- Identify quick wins, quick improvements
- Implement Agile practices: adaptability, communication, KPIs

Define and Understand How the Value Streams

- Understand and improve the processes
- Introduce Short term alignment practices
- Introduce value stream mapping

Innovate and Design

- Understand variation
- Compensate for variation
- Reduce variation: VOC, process mapping, analysis
- Learn from the hidden champions

Optimize the Flow

- Work to takt time
- Build models for the key processes

Become Demand Focused

- Plan for every request
- Introduce Pull
- Foster a culture of continuous progress

Total People Involvement   Voice of the Customer, Employees, Partners

Chapter 13 -Conclusion

As a conclusion to this book, we would like to leave you with twenty-one key takeaways to consider as you navigate your journey toward achieving excellence or transformation. These takeaways are presented in the order they appeared in the book.

1. **The changing landscape of the modern workplace**: The new generations of employees, such as millennials and Gen Z, have distinct characteristics and expectations from the traditional workforce. They value technology, diversity, flexibility, purpose, and feedback. They seek workplaces that align with their personal values and identity. We can motivate and retain younger workers by providing career growth and learning opportunities, offering work-life balance and remote work options, articulating the impact and mission of the work, giving personalized and meaningful recognition, and fostering a culture of open dialogue and transparency.

2. **The evolution of customer expectations:** These expectations have changed since the pandemic, especially in terms of speed, convenience, and quality of service.

3. **The role of technology and automation in the digital age**: Technology and automation have transformed the workplace and the customer experience and can increase productivity, quality, efficiency, cost savings, safety, scalability, and flexibility. However, there are some drawbacks, such as job displacement, initial implementation costs, technical challenges, limitations, reduced human interaction, and dependency on technology. This book also raises the question of whether to automate or redesign processes first.

4. **The need for a nuanced and adaptive approach to management**: Managers need to develop strong people management and development skills, lead by example, and be

authentic and transparent. We must avoid cookie-cutter approaches and instead be flexible and innovative.

5. **The challenges of hiring and retaining employees for SMBs**: They face competition from larger companies that can offer better salaries and benefits, as well as more brand recognition and job security. SMBs need to communicate their mission and vision clearly to attract and engage employees.

6. **The need for flexibility and agility for SMBs**: They need to adapt to changing customer needs and market opportunities; this can be achieved by having a low level of fixed costs, a shallow organizational structure, and a responsive decision-making process.

7. **The difference between growing wide and deep in the market**: Growing wide means expanding the customer base and reaching new markets, while growing deep means increasing sales and loyalty within the existing customer base. Both strategies have advantages and disadvantages depending on the business's goals and resources.

8. **The importance of cash and working capital**: Cash and working capital are crucial for the smooth operation and growth of a business. A healthy level of cash and working capital is essential for a business to meet its short-term obligations and avoid bankruptcy.

9. **The importance of putting customers and employees first**: To achieve quick wins and improvements, managers should involve customers and employees in the process and create a solid foundation for engagement and culture.

10. **The benefits and challenges of flat organizational structures**: They can promote a culture of collaboration and trust among team members, as well as increase efficiency, agility, and flexibility. However, flat structures can also create confusion, conflicts, and lack of clarity.

11. **Start with simple methods and frameworks for identifying and eliminating waste**: Use the SWOT analysis, Benefit vs. Effort Matrix, SCAMPER, and team huddles. These methods and

frameworks can help improve the value and quality of their products and services.

12. **The importance of documenting and aligning the processes**: Documenting the processes concisely, such as a procedure or a work instruction, helps to create a collective understanding and standard for everyone involved.

13. **Use the Lean Six Sigma methodology:** Use it to reduce waste and variation and improve quality and efficiency. It incorporates many tools, including brainstorming, affinity diagram, Ishikawa diagram, five why analysis, process mapping, and value stream mapping.

14. **Process mapping and value stream mapping are needed**: This is a tool to document and analyze the current state of a process and to identify improvement opportunities and root causes of problems. By mapping out the steps, inputs, outputs, roles, and resources involved in a process, one can identify gaps, bottlenecks, redundancies, or delays that impact the quality, speed, or cost of the process.

15. **We can compensate for or reduce variation**: Sorting, selection, inspection, poka yoke, and statistical analysis are some ways to cope with, reduce, or eliminate variation in the process output.

16. **Learn from the hidden champions**: There are always firms or individuals that innovate ahead of the market and create solutions for their own needs, often without being aware of their potential value to others.

17. **Enable processes and people to work to takt time:** Work balancing is the process of distributing the workload across different steps or stations in a process to ensure that each step operates at the same pace and meets the takt time. Single request flow is the practice of working on one request or service at a time instead of batching.

18. **Process modelling is a way to optimize the process**. It can involve different techniques, such as value stream mapping, regression analysis, simulation, or machine learning.

19. **Becoming demand-focused becomes more important with time:** We need to establish a strategy to accept or refuse the upcoming demands from customers that may require customization or adaptation. Variety and customization are ways to offer different options or features for a product or service that cater to different tastes and preferences. They require optimized processes, tools, and systems to reduce costs and waste.

20. **Pull enables being demand-focused**: A pull delivery system is one in which products or services are produced or delivered on demand based on the actual needs or orders of customers. It reduces inventory, waste, and overproduction. To implement it, organizations need to coordinate and communicate among the various parts of the processes, using visual management tools such as kanban boards or signals.

21. **The circular economy is coming to town**: It relates to demand because it responds to the growing environmental and social concerns of customers and stakeholders and offers new opportunities for value creation, differentiation, and innovation.

As J.R.R. Tolkien once said, "The greatest adventure is what lies ahead". Our delight and fulfilment come not only from achieving our ultimate goals but also from navigating the path to get there. After all, our aspirations evolve because change is woven into our being.

Wishing you a magnificent, blissful, and fruitful odyssey.

Index

About the Author

Alex Boussetta, P. Eng. M. Eng., PMP, CM&A, Agile SMC,
DASSM, PCCP, EP, CES
Certified Lean Six Sigma Master Black Belt
Partner, Executive Consultant. Operational Excellence
Abacus Team Inc.

Alex Boussetta, a renowned industry leader with over three decades of elite operational experience, has carved out a successful career embodying transformative leadership and cutting-edge innovation. As an alumnus of the New York Institute of Finance, and the Massachusetts Institute of Technology (MIT), Boussetta has cultivated an extensive repertoire of knowledge, receiving a Masters in Engineering Project Management, along with Professional Certifications in Innovation and Technology, Machine Learning and Artificial Intelligence, Advanced Design and Manufacturing. He is as well an

Environmental Professional and a Circular Economy Specialist.

Throughout his career, Alex has driven organizational advancement by effectively managing global matrix structures, taking charge of strategic responsibility and P&L. His leadership portfolio is diverse, stretching across sectors from aerospace to manufacturing, healthcare, and government. Notable past roles include spearheading the Six Sigma Competency Center at Bombardier Aerospace as Manager, steering operational efficiency as Corporate Director of Lean at MAAX, and overseeing quality and supply chain dynamics as Director at Blackberry.

Alex's passion for fostering operational excellence has led him to establish Abacus Team Inc., a consultancy committed to driving quality in start-ups and industry giants alike. This venture embodies his experience and insights drawn from managing company transformations and turnaround initiatives.

Alex has spent two decades imparting his wisdom to the next generation of leaders at McGill University. As the Program Leader for Operational Excellence, he is shaping curricula and guiding minds in Lean Six Sigma, Agile Project Management, and Operations Management, while also serving as the Advanced Management Program Advisor for the McGill Executive Institute.

Over the years, he has trained, coached, and certified over 1,400 Green Belts and Lean experts, alongside 280 Black Belts and 21 Master Black Belts, demonstrating his immense influence in the field.

A Certified Lean Six Sigma Master Black Belt, Lean Sensei, Project Management Professional (PMP), Agile SCRUM Master (SMC) and a Prosci Certified Change Practitioner (PCCP), Alex is well-respected in the industry, demonstrated by his VIP award from General Electric, Five Star Award from Blackberry, and McGill Dean's Service Award for Outstanding Contribution. His impactful contributions to project management and design, alongside product and services breakthroughs, set him apart as an influential thought leader and an inspiring role model.